Belonging

S. D. Gaede

Belonging

Academie
Books Michigan Grand Rapids,
Zondervan Publishing House

BELONGING:
OUR NEED FOR COMMUNITY IN CHURCH AND FAMILY
Copyright © 1985 by The Zondervan Corporation
Grand Rapids, Michigan

ACADEMIE BOOKS is an imprint of
Zondervan Publishing House 1415 Lake Drive, SE
Grand Rapids, Michigan 49506

Library of Congress Cataloging in Publication Data

Gaede, S. D.
  Belonging.
  1. Christian communities.   2. Community.
3. Civilization, Modern—1950–.   I. Title.
BV4405.G34   1985   260   85-17987
ISBN   0–310–36891–X

Edited by Gerard Terpstra

Printed in the United States of America

87 88 89 90 91 / 10 9 8 7 6 5 4 3 2

For Judy

to whom
by the grace of God
I belong

Contents

V. THE FAITHFUL COMMUNITY

VI. THE INTIMATE COMMUNITY

VII. MODERNITY AT BAY: COMMUNITY EXPRESSED

Preface

What follows is a most peculiar treatise, fitting few of the categories we like to use to discover an author's intent. Its contents may appear academic, but it has been written for the layman. It is imbued with sociological insights, but it is not a study in sociology. It is rooted in Christian assumptions, but it is certainly not a discourse in theology. It attempts to focus on the topic of "community," but few terms in the English language are more ambiguous. Altogether, it would seem to be a most confusing enterprise. And yet its contents flow from my soul with the ease of an unbridled brook, neither hesitant about its source nor concerned about the topographer's description.

This book, then, is a personal statement. It is, to be more precise, a personal expression of concern about the condition of human communities in the modern world. Thus it comes not so much from a specific academic discipline as it does from a particular heart. Hearts, however, are not without their passions, and books founded on them are rarely lacking in rhetorical exaggeration. This book is no exception. No doubt, those scholars whose fields are touched upon most directly will feel the pain of this hyperbole most intensely. Nevertheless, the purpose of this book is not to satisfy the scholar with details, but to present—as forcefully as possible—the broad contours of a general argument. For that reason I have eschewed much of the language and style of scholarly discourse, omitting the standard plethora of references, footnotes, and statistics.

Lack of references, however, should lead no one to think that in writing this book I incurred no debts. There are many whose thoughts have informed my own, and in the pages that follow, one will find telltale signs of Peter Berger, John Calvin, Emile Durkheim, Jacques Ellul, Robert Nisbet, David Riesman, Menno Simons, Ferdinand Tonnies, and Max Weber. Especially evident are the contributions of Judy Gaede, Robert Clark, and David Wells. To all these, and many others who must remain unnamed, I am deeply grateful.

Two final comments. First, though modernity comes off badly in this book, no one should assume that I am either unappreciative of its benefits or believe that its precursor was without fault. I too live in the modern world. I have enjoyed its many choices and opportunities, and I would not give them up to live in a preindustrialized society. But in saying this, I am like the child who has lived with overly indulgent parents; although I know the delights they offer are not always in my best interest, I would not think of trading my parents in for stricter models. They are, after all, *my* parents. The question is, Will I be sage enough to refuse those gifts that may bring me to ruin? Few children would be able to exercise such wisdom. Therefore I worry about the children of modernity.

Finally, a word about existential sources: Some books are born in response to an unfulfilled personal need and a craving to have that need met. This book is not one of them. There can be no doubt that I have been blessed with the gift of durable relationships. From the days of my youth until the present, I have been a member of genuine communities of faith and intimacy. For this, of course, there can be no human accounting; such communities are a rarity in the modern world. I come to the topic of "community," then, not as one who is outside, but as one who has been blessed beyond measure in a world without blessing. My burden is not that of the starving, but of the well-nourished who must regularly peer into the eyes of the anemic. I must frankly admit that, if my God would let me do so, I would gladly recline in the luxury of my riches. But, alas, his blessings do not arrive untethered with responsibilities, nor without the hope of better worlds to come.

PART I / The Problem Defined

one / The Problem of Community

Student walked into my office the other day to lay out his plan for radical social change. He wanted to abolish the March Thaw. Student is a nice fellow. A junior sociology major from New Jersey, he is bright, articulate, and thoroughly disgusted with the social arrangements that characterize his existence.

He has come to discover that much of his life is encumbered by roles and values that no longer have meaning for him. His church is endlessly embroiled in controversies about budget and growth, and seems totally oblivious to the wretched of the earth that live right next door. His parents, who have just managed to taste the affluence of the American middle class, are absorbed in the values of clean home, clean car, and clean body. His friends have dedicated themselves to the pursuit of M.D.s, M.B.A.s, and B.V.D.s (the "abundant life" as they call it) and seem absolutely impervious to the moans of the oppressed, the sick, and the afflicted. And his college—his *Christian* college, which charges an exorbitant tuition for his attendance—has succumbed to the values of his church, parents, and friends. Clear evidence of that fact is the mere existence of the "March Thaw."

The March Thaw is a college tradition. It is the one time in the year when students get all gussied up, drive to one of Boston's finest, and are treated to an evening of exquisite dining and entertainment. Accordingly, it is expensive—for the student and the college. And it is this fact that so disgusts my student.

"Here we are," he complains, "throwing away thousands of dollars so that a hotel can make money, we can stuff our stomachs, and everyone can feel copacetic. What about those who are hungry, who have nothing at all to eat? How can we dine like kings and cast a blind eye at those who have such needs? What right do we have to use God's good earth for our pleasure when there are millions in pain and agony?" To Student, the answer is clear: we cannot. We must immediately dispense with the March Thaw and donate the proceeds to UNICEF. There simply is no "Christian" alternative.

Now why should Student wish to inform me of all these things? Because I am his principal instructor in such matters. I am the Christian sociologist who enticed him into the discipline as a freshman with reams of material on poverty, repression, and Christian responsibility. It was I who told him of the anguish in Appalachia, the malnutrition in Mexico, and the rot in Roxbury. It was I who explained the social exigencies

14

that give rise to such calamities and enlightened him on their costs and consequences for the human spirit. And it was I who spat out verse after biblical verse concerning the Christian's responsibilities to the needy. "Nothing is clearer in the biblical record," I would say confidently, "than God's concern for the poor." Student was my protégé; I, his mentor. And Student had learned his lessons well.

What Student did not know, however, was that his mentor had six years before been the dean of students and, as such, had been responsible for the ongoing development and enhancement of the March Thaw. He came into my office expecting to find a sympathetic ear and, perhaps, a bit of advice. What he received, instead, was a series of impertinent questions.

Value of Tradition

"Tell me, Student," I said, "what is your responsibility to the past?"

"What do you mean?" he asked with a somewhat quizzical look on his face.

"I mean," I said, as I sat back deeply into my arm chair, "I mean, what is your obligation to those who have trod these hallowed halls before you—to those who have established traditions and symbols and certain ways of doing things in this community? What is your responsibility to them?"

"Alive or dead?" he snapped with all the aggressiveness of an amateur boxer.

"Either," I replied.

"Nothing to the dead," he responded quickly. And then after a moment's reflection: "I suppose I owe an explanation now and then to the living, but I am primarily responsible to myself—to do things as I think they ought to be done." He paused for just a moment and then retrieved the boxer motif. "I know what you're driving at. You like the March Thaw for some

15

unknown reason, and you're hoping to justify it by saying that I have some vague responsibility to the past. Well, I don't—at least, not if it means the perpetuation of injustice!" With this last jab, Student was clearly pleased. He had walked into the ring unaware that there was to be a fight, but the moment he sensed opposition, he came out with elbows up and nostrils flaring. Stimulated by the competition, I decided to pursue him with a second question: "What did you have for lunch today, my friend?"

"What?" he said, as he cast his eyes about, looking for time to plumb my intentions.

"Lunch, ol' man! What did you eat?" I snapped.

"Hamburger, Coke, and french fries," he said, giving up on his attempt to decipher my motives.

"How in good conscience could you perpetrate such an injustice on the hungry of the world?" I said, mimicking the tones he had successfully used a few moments before.

"That's different than the March Thaw," he burst out, "and you know it!"

"Why?" I said softly; there was no need to use the right hook when the left jab was working so effectively.

"It's a matter of degree," he continued. "I could save maybe a dollar by purchasing a cheaper lunch, but we could save thousands of dollars by not holding the March Thaw."

"I understand that a dollar can feed a Third World child for almost a week," I said, enjoying myself immensely. "Seems pretty significant to me."

"Look, Professor, what are you driving at?" he complained. "What is the bottom line?"

"One more question," I said, as I looked purposefully around his glare. "What is your responsibility to the future?"

"Oh, good gravy!" he moaned. "What in the world do you mean by that?"

"What kind of responsibility do you have to those who will come after you at this institution?" I harped unangelically. Knowing full well what I meant, but needing more time, he quipped, "I still don't understan

"I know," I said, lowering my voice into a modulated professorial tone (something of a cross between a parent's and a dictator's—always detested it myself, but this seemed the right moment for such a tactic). "That's the lesson you missed. You have remembered your responsibility to the poor. You have remembered your responsibility to your own convictions. But you have forgotten your responsibility to the community of which you are a part.

"You know what I think?" I continued after a short interlude. "Way down deep in the bowels of your consciousness, you think the whole universe revolves around you and your pet concerns. As a result, you believe that the community will be better off if it ignores its past and invests its future in your hands. But what gives you the right to deny to the students of the future the traditions of the past? Do your obviously legitimate concerns for the poor and oppressed obviate the needs of others for special events, good fellowship, and aesthetic experiences?"

PRIORITY OF VALUES

It was a heavy blow and it clearly surprised him. Because I was not the kind to make direct frontal attacks, my assertion that his attitudes were essentially selfish caught him a bit off guard. He paused for a moment, but quickly regained his composure.

"Wait just a minute," he asserted with some authority. "I'm not against traditions. But I don't think they have any intrinsic value either. The issue here is one of justice. If a tradition serves that purpose, then fine. But if not—if it becomes a vehicle for the perpetration of injustice—then it is a problem and it ought to be changed or discarded. Justice is the issue," he repeated with self-righteous glee, "not tradition!"

It was an excellent point. The value of tradition can never hold up against the value of justice, and if that were the only matter at stake here, his argument would clearly win the day. It was apparent that if I was to have any success at all in this venture, I would have to get even more personal.

"Really?" I said softly. "Do you *really* believe that justice is the only issue here?" I asked, increasing the volume a bit. "You're concerned that students will spend fifteen dollars on a nice evening out, right? You think that is unjust because they could eat for a fifth of that cost at the dining hall, right? Remember the other day when I went over to your room to pick up that book you borrowed from my office three years ago? Didn't I see a stereo system there worth at least three to four hundred dollars? Tell me, how can you justify such an expenditure considering the needs of the world's poor? I mean, do you *really* need that piece of equipment more than they need food? And don't you have a car? My goodness, how can you possibly *drive* when millions all over the globe can't even *walk* because they are so malnourished? And what about that Lacoste you're wearing, not to mention that ring on your finger and those Weejuns on your feet? *How can you do that*, ol' man?" I said with ever-increasing volume.

After a deep breath and a sympathetic glance at his perturbed but undaunted countenance, I continued the monologue. "Look, Student, I don't know why you possess all these things, but I suspect it is because they are of value to you. For one reason or another, you have decided that despite the poor in Panama and the beggars in Boston these things are worth the cost—to your pocketbook as well as your conscience.

The real issue here, the crux of the problem, is that your stereo is worth it to you and the March Thaw is not. That's, as you say, the bottom line, isn't it? I must admit I find that interesting, particularly since the March Thaw is a voluntary event. No one is requiring you to spend your money that way—you don't have to attend or in any way associate yourself with the thing. But that's not good enough for you, is it? You want to take away the March Thaw from everyone else, as well. Your sense of justice assumes that no one ought to be allowed to participate in the event. Why is that, do you suppose?

"Let me be so bold as to suggest an answer," I continued. "You have no sense of responsibility to this community. Your world is consumed by your interests and your interests alone. In this case, your interests are lofty ones. What could be more important than the needs of the poor? It is a qualitatively good thing to be concerned about the poor! Moreover, it is a very difficult thing indeed to wrestle with the question of one's responsibility to the poor as a wealthy Westerner. Most of us do not wrestle with it just *because* it is so debilitating. I am glad you're not like that; I am glad that you're concerned about the issue. But as you contemplate serving the needy who are removed from you, please—please don't forget to serve those who eat, drink, and live with you."

PRECARIOUS COMMUNITY

Needless to say, the mood in my office had become a somber one. It was now clear that the issue was one that was deeply personal for both of us. For that reason, I suppose, I had done the unpardonable: I had attacked his character. I had questioned his motivations and accused him of hypocrisy. Obviously, he was not pleased. Neither was I. Somehow, I needed to depersonalize the topic a bit, or I was going to lose him—not only in debate, but also as a friend.

19

"Look here," I murmured in a softer, more dispassionate tone, "as a member of this community, you have a great deal of power. Unfortunately, almost all of it is destructive in nature. You represent a link in a chain of community experiences. You are a small link, to be sure. Indeed, looking at the chain as a whole, you are hardly visible. But as a small link, you hold together past and future generations of this community. It will take all of your courage, ability and imagination to simply play your part—just to hold onto those rather small links beside you. But it takes only a little weakness, a careless act, a whimsical gesture, to break the chain. Forever.

"It isn't difficult to throw away a tradition, you know. Just sell your brand of justice—or whatever other ideal you may choose—to enough people at the same time, and they will gladly dispose of a tradition. But have you ever tried to *start* one? Have you ever tried to *build* a community? *You* can't do it, you know. It isn't something that one link can accomplish. It happens only after a variety of men and women, with a host of different gifts and abilities, have spent enormous amounts of time and effort trying to be true to one another and a few cherished values. It takes years to build—years of repetition, endurance, and patience. And it can all vanish. In a flash."

We sat there in awkward silence for a few seconds (the kind of seconds that feel like hours). Eventually, he looked up from the floor, possessing a semicocky smile. It was a smile that told me that we were still friends but that he had every intention of remaining my intellectual equal.

"You know what I think?" he said in a voice that matched his smile precisely. "Exactly the same thing I thought five minutes ago. I think you like the March Thaw and you're trying to rationalize it with an ethereal concept of 'community.' I think you care about fine food and good entertainment more that you care about the poor and the oppressed. And I suspect that you are doing exactly what you have accused me of doing: justifying your own personal interests."

THE COMMUNITY VALUED

Student did not use as many words as I, but he used them to better effect. Once again, in the span of two sentences, he had cut through my verbiage with a rather precise analysis of the problem. And I knew, moreover, that he was probably correct.

I paused a moment, heaved a heavy sigh, and admitted the checkmate. "I suppose," I started, then stopped, and then began again, "I suppose, Student, you are right. I suspect that I am rationalizing my love of the good life through my appreciation of the community. And that's really the tragedy, isn't it? 'Community' is the kind of concept that can be used to cover a multitude of sins. Hitler used it to justify aggression. Jim Jones used it to effect a mass slaughter. The church has used it time and time again to protect error and resist change. And I—I have probably used it to cover up my own irresponsibility. It seems that every time—"

A knock at the door interrupted my confession. Before I had a chance to yell "Come in," a second student burst through the doorway.

"Let's go!" yelled Student #2 to Student #1. "The coach said we had to be dressed for the basketball game by 5:00, and it's already 4:45!"

"You're kidding," blurted Student #1 in disbelief as he anxiously looked down at his watch. "I completely forgot! I'm sorry, professor, I really must go. Thanks for the chat and all," he said, more out of good upbringing than feeling.

"Important game tonight?" I asked, similarly on the basis of parental training.

21

"The biggest!" he said as he slipped toward the door. "We're playing Prince of Peace College. They're huge, they're undefeated, and they play with a real evangelical zeal!" By this he meant that they were as rough on the court as we were.

"Well, good luck," I said as I walked to the door behind him. And then, as an afterthought: "Uh—do you think anyone will show up for the game?"

"Are you kidding?" he said in startled surprise. "The gym will be packed out!"

"But, what if. . . ?" I said as I caught his glance, "what if you walked out onto the gym floor this evening and there wasn't one solitary soul sitting in the bleachers?"

"Professor!" he started, with some irritation and with great incredulity, "that just wouldn't happen. This is it! This is *the* game of the year! Don't you know . . . that . . . ?" And then suddenly he stopped talking, and one of those rare moments occurred when eyeball meets eyeball and student meets professor. It is the kind of moment that every professor covets, the kind that carries one through those interminable blue books, sleepy-eyed audiences, and inane faculty meetings. Nothing was said, but more communication took place within that moment than in all my babblings the entire week.

"Come on!" said Student #2, who reappeared impatiently at the door. *"We've gotta go!"*

"Must go, professor," said the somewhat subdued voice of Student #1. "Are you coming to the game?" he asked without much reflection.

"I wouldn't miss it for the world!" I responded, as I slipped back toward my chair in fatigued rapture.

THE PROBLEM OF COMMUNITY

Community. It is a peculiar concept. To some it is a rather stodgy term, indicating a matter of fact (e.g., "I live in the community of Hamilton"). To others, however, community connotes a state of being or a quality of life, relating more to feelings than geographical fact (e.g., "There isn't a sense of community in this church!"). Still, for others, community is both fact and feeling, describing an arrangement of human relationships that can either add to or diminish the quality of one's existence. For those subscribing to this latter notion, the battle between the first two conceptions of community is a bit odd and more than a little disconcerting. It is rather like arguing whether "love" is a noun or a verb. If either party ever won such an argument, the human race would be the loser.

What the reader holds in hand is a discussion of community in its most global and, to some people, vulgar form. It assumes that community is a "thing," yet not just a thing; an "experience," yet not just an experience. The first point means that when we discuss community, we are ruminating about an object that is material and can be perceived with the senses. The second, however, suggests it is also something that one can feel from the heart—to enjoy or endure, to cling to or rebel against, to rest in or wrestle with, to experience or fail to experience.

It is the possibility of failure that particularly concerns me. It is disturbing because I think we need community (in the broadest sense) in order to be the kind of people God intended. Without it we are impoverished; without it the human race is in serious difficulty. It concerns me as well because fewer and fewer of us are truly active participants in community. Especially for those of us who find ourselves in the "modern" world (the world of high technology and high living), community is a commodity in short supply. Indeed, we live in a society where social structures may obstruct community and people have little notion of what genuine community entails. Like the student in my office, we have come to believe that community is a tool to be used or discarded as we see fit. It is a means, a piece of technology, an impediment to be eliminated or a convenience to be manipulated for our own pleasure. Community is, today, conceived of as something we choose. And the choice is not only "which" but "whether."

Unfortunately (or fortunately, depending on one's point of departure), such is not the case. Community is not a personal choice; it is a given. It is a gift that a coterie of people may impart to one another but none can independently choose. Its existence is contingent on, among other things, the willingness of the body to adopt the member. An individual may choose to be a part of a community from now until the last trumpet, but the choice will be futile unless the community embraces the suppliant. The tragedy, of course, is that we are constantly told otherwise. Indeed, we are not only exhorted to "choose" our communities these days, we are compelled to do so. It is one of the more interesting dilemmas of modernity that it has made a necessity out of an impossibility.

At one level, of course, the problem of community is simply a problem of trust. This because a prerequisite of community is trust—not blind trust, not idolatrous trust, but a trust that assumes that I am accountable to and for my neighbor. Such an assumption allows me to plod through life with the assurance that if I have exceptional needs, significant others will come to my aid. This kind of trust is based, not on altruism, but on a recognition of the human condition—that we mortals need one another in order to be fully human. It is this kind of trust that guards against the excesses of self-interest and individualistic greed. It is a kind of trust that is almost totally lacking in our life together today.

At another level, however, the problem of community is a problem of faith. We do not have community because we do not have trust; but we do not trust because we lack sufficient motivation. In other words, we have no reason to trust. For trust to survive, it must be rooted in deep faith—a faith that stretches one beyond one's petty interests and self preoccupations and points one toward a reality larger than oneself. But like the trust that it shoulders, deep faith is conspicuous by its absence in the modern world.

Especially on this point, I wish not to be misunderstood. It is not that we moderns are a people without faith, or a people unable to believe. Indeed, we have our gods and idols in gargantuan proportions. But our faith is invested in nothing beyond our immediate environment. Its purview is defined by our appetites, its depth measured by the moment. While such a faith can be very exhausting and can, no doubt, tap our passions, it can never produce the kind of trust necessary for the full flowering of community. Whatever else a community may need, surely this is foundational—a faith rooted in something vaster than oneself.

All of this suggests that we live in a world that radically undermines precisely the community it so desperately needs. At least, that is the hypothesis of this book. First, it is my conviction that modernity makes the "fact and feeling" of community a near impossibility. As we will see, it does this by subverting the core ingredients of community—relationships, traditions, and vision. Second, I believe that humanity requires a healthy community for its general well-being. This assumption is rooted in the type of creatures we are as well as the type of Creator it is whose hand gives us our form. Finally, however, I believe it is not enough merely to attempt an understanding of the problem; rather, we must begin the process of correcting it. That is, we must be about the business of creating communities—both for the well-

being of our species and the glory of our Creator—
even in the midst of modernity.

FUTURE AGENDA

Such is the task of this treatise. Not a modest
agenda, to be sure. To understand the inscrutable predilections of modern society relative to community, is,
of itself, more than a challenge. To offer suggestions
for the future development of religious and family
communities, based on that understanding, is clearly
hazardous business. But to do so using the prose of
the English language rather than the rubric of acade-
mia, is perilous at best, and, quite possibly, foolish.
Nevertheless, persuaded more by the need for the
project than the wisdom of its doing, these shall remain my objectives. In pursuing these goals, four
questions will guide our discussion. First, what is the
problem of community in the modern world? Second,
how has it found expression within the spheres of
religion and family? Third, of what significance is the
problem of community for the Christian? And fourth,
how can we build genuine communities of faith and
intimacy in the modern world? While the heart and
mind may ache from such questions, in them the pen
delights.

two / The Problem of Modernity

A court case was presented on television the other day. It depicted a situation in which a young woman, having dinner at a restaurant one night, suddenly found herself choking on a piece of food. With the food lodged firmly in her throat, she was unable to breathe or speak. Desperately she pointed out her predicament to her friends sharing the dinner table, but they were immobilized by uncertainty, responding only in shrieks and panic.

Another patron in the restaurant, noticing that she was choking and that none of her friends were dealing with the problem, quickly grabbed her by the shoulders, lifted her to a standing position, and applied the Heimlich maneuver in order to dislodge the piece of food. Although he had gone through a course of study covering this particular medical procedure, he apparently used it incorrectly. As a result, though he was able to dislodge the food, he also damaged the woman's kidney and spleen. In effect, he saved her life but, in the process, caused her severe bodily injury.

This case came to court when the woman brought suit against the man who rescued her, claiming that he had acted without due care and without her consent. From her perspective, his improper use of the Heimlich maneuver had ruined her life. Regardless of his good intentions, he had had no right to intervene in her affairs in this manner. He owed her for damages and a good bit more.

In the court scene, recreated for television, the jurors were allowed to discuss the case with the program moderator. Through that discussion, it became evident that the jurors had mixed opinions as to the appropriate verdict. Some thought she deserved to win the suit, pointing out that the man acted impulsively and without discretion. They thought he had no right to perform such a dangerous procedure on the woman without her consent. Others, on the other hand, thought he had acted in good faith, attempting to rescue the life of the woman; they pointed out that he had actually succeeded in saving her life, even though damage was done in the process. For that damage, however, they thought he should not be held accountable.

As I listened to the presentation of this case, I was struck not so much by the arguments pro and con, but by the existential fact of the case itself. In some societies, the man would have been considered a hero—a savior of sorts. In others, his action would have been perceived as unexceptional and hardly worth commendation. But in ours, the man was in the dock. He was neither normal nor exemplary. He was suspect.

It is important to see that this is not just the case of an unappreciative individual who is more concerned with the possibility of monetary gain than the necessity of gratitude. As repulsive as her selfish ambition may be, it is not the big story here. The critical thing to note is that her plea for "justice" is predicated on her right to be independent—to be free of interference from others, even if the interference is intended to save her life.

Such a plea makes sense in our society, only because the autonomy of the individual is valued more highly than our communal responsibilities to one another. For that reason, no thought was given to bringing suit against those friends who sat watching the women choke and did nothing to help. In our society, they are not open to the charge of "irresponsibility," and, indeed, to us such a suit would seem ludicrous. But the man who acted—who was presumptuous enough to involve himself in the life of this woman *without asking her permission*—he is the one whose behavior is questionable, regardless of how noble his intentions. It is the good Samaritan who worries us, not the priest or the Levite.

The question is, Why? Why is communal responsibility taken so lightly? And why is the individual's autonomy so vigorously defended? To answer such questions, we must understand the nature of modern society.

MODERNITY

The facts of modernity, of course, are neither novel nor especially entertaining. We have heard most of them before, and the human mind is dulled by repetition. That is unfortunate, because the facts of modernity are important. Perhaps the best angle on our world, however, is achieved when looked at from the perspective of a more traditional society. Instead of taking the twentieth century as our point of departure, therefore, let us initiate our discussion of modernity with a brief tour of a hypothetical hamlet in eleventh-century Europe.

Antiquity. If we moderns were to walk through such a hamlet, we would no doubt first be struck by the paucity of technological gadgetry in that community— the lack of conveniences (toilets, electricity, indoor plumbing, etc.) and techniques (food distribution and storage, for example). But if our vision went further, we would see a number of other striking features about the village and the lives of its inhabitants.

First, as we enter, we may be amazed simply by the size of the town. By modern standards, it looks small—very small. As a result, when we begin to interact with the villagers, we may note that their experiences with people and things beyond their town is quite limited. Almost everyone in the hamlet, for example, probably speaks only one language (except possibly a merchant or two), and they are deeply suspicious of those of foreign tongue.

As we talk with them about their work, we discover that rare is the individual who has ever had a job different from the one he or she is now performing. Moreover, that job, we find, consumes the better part of their day. Sunlight is for work, and, except for an occasional festival or wedding (and, of course, the Sabbath), waking hours are devoted to the task of maintaining life. Although these folk do not seem to go about their daily tasks at the speed we moderns are accustomed to, they nevertheless are engaged in job-related activities almost continuously.

Should we pursue our investigation in greater depth, we would discover that three institutions dominate the lives of these peasant folk. First, there are family or kinship ties that structure their daily interaction patterns. These are the relationships that are primary in their lives, and they extend beyond the home and into the job, the market, and virtually everywhere else. Second, there is the institution of the church, whose values and organizational tentacles reach into every corner of the village. The church's influence is pervasive, and its pronouncements and judgments affect what goes on in the public world of the job and government, as well as in the private domain of marriage, family, and friendships. Finally, there is the state, which, though small by modern standards, is generally authoritative in its sphere. The state maintains its power by physical force as well as by the force of tradition (e.g., royal lineage), and the common folk do not feel that they have (or should have) much influence on its behavior. The church, on the other hand, does have some influence over the state and the state is normally required to work out a rapprochement with the church—one that involves a kind of "bargain of power."

Modernity. Even from this brief sketch of life in an eleventh-century village, it is not difficult to see the marked contrast between that community and those of our own era. Most of us modern types, for example, live in towns or cities that are huge by comparison. In our society it is the exceptional individual who resides in a small community.

Moreover, the people with whom we interact are not necessarily like us—physically or culturally. Some of them speak other languages and have a heritage that is significantly different from our own. Though we moan about the ethnocentric American who knows only a homespun version of English, the fact is that most of us assume it is "too bad" that we are not bilingual. We stand in awe of those who travel extensively and are familiar with a variety of cultures and languages. This is not to say that we moderns are less prejudiced and bigoted than our eleventh-century compatriots were. We are not. We are, however, less inclined to think that a different culture is evil simply because it is different (we come up with other reasons for intolerance). Through the media as well as daily interaction, we are exposed to people whose lives and perspectives on life diverge from our own.

Another contrasting feature of modernity relates to the arena of work. Whereas the eleventh-century villager spends most of his or her time earning a subsistence living, we moderns invest a relatively small amount of time on the job. Not only do we have more vacations and longer weekends (made, we are told, for Michelob), but we also have much shorter working days. All of this means that we spend much more time in nonvocational activities. For the middle class, this translates into more leisure time (for travel, sports, and entertainment), while for the lower class this may mean a second job or more time to contemplate one's navel, one's poverty, or both. Not only do we have more time away from work, but we are also involved in a panoply of occupations. There are literally millions of different kinds of jobs in the modern city; at times we find it very difficult even to explain to one another what we do to earn a living. (It is not unusual these days to meet people who find it virtually impossible to explain the purpose or function of their spouse's vocation.)

Institutionally, as well, we live in a much more variegated and heterogeneous world. Many of the responsibilities of the church and the family, for instance, have been taken over by other institutions in the modern society. Not only do we have "churches" rather than a "church," but institutional religion's sphere of influence has waned considerably. Certainly, it no longer has the political clout it once had, nor does it have as much influence on the private lives of its parishioners (not to mention the fact that many modern types are *not* parishioners).

The state, on the other hand, is much larger and more diffuse in the modern world, with agencies and regulations that pervade the life of the society. Although we moderns debate the value of the bureaucratic state, we have nevertheless come to depend on it for education, welfare, and economic stability. Clearly, the state has taken over many of the functions of the family and the church.

Numerous institutions, however, have been established to accomplish the tasks once performed by the groups formed by the bonds of kinship and religion—counseling services, disaster relief, welfare services, retirement programs, elderly assistance, etc. Some of these are government-sponsored while others depend on private philanthropy (or some combination of the two), but all of them function outside of the traditional sovereignty of the family and church (even those funded by religious organizations usually operate independent of the parent denomination). What this means is that our daily lives are dominated much more extensively by a variety of *public* institutions than was the case for the villager in eleventh-century Europe.

Such contrasts between what some would call "pre-industrial" and "industrial" societies are, of course, a bit of an exaggeration. Were a European historian to read over the last few pages, he or she would probably say that I have exaggerated the isolation of the villager, just as a contemporary sociologist might claim that I have embellished the heterogeneity of modernity (or its effects on the life of the individual). If they are worth their salt, however, they will admit that the general picture is correct—the world of moderns is substantially more varied, public, and pluralistic than that of our ancestors.

The key point, then, is that much of the Western world has moved (especially over the last few centuries) from the life of the villager to the life of the modern urban/suburbanite—from folk society to urban society (Redfield), from mechanical solidarity to organic solidarity (Durkheim), from *gemeinschaft* to *gesellschaft* (Toennies), from tradition-directed through inner-directed to other-directed lives (Riesman), from alienation to *anomie* (Berger), ad infinitum. Few social changes are better documented than this one, and few are more important. It is the shift known as "modernization."

RELATIONSHIPS

Now all of this seems quite matter of fact and rather unexceptional until one investigates the impact of this modernization process on human beings. What we must keep in mind, and what we moderns find so difficult to appreciate, is that this process did not happen merely to things. It does not simply mean that toilets (or their equivalents) went from outside to in, or that jobs went from the farm to the city, or that transportation went from animal to mechanical. It happened to *people*. Not only did people develop the techniques that changed *things*, but the "things" people created changed these people's lives.

One of those changes occurred in the domain of relationships. Peter Peasant (as we will call our eleventh-century villager) lived in one community his entire life. It was the rare individual who moved his place of residence in Peter's society. Much more likely was the possibility that Peter would live in one section of one community throughout his life cycle, regardless of ambition or marital status. This meant that Peter knew personally most of the people with whom he came into contact on a daily basis. His relationships—on the job, in the marketplace, or at church—were all quite familiar to him.

What this does not suggest is that all of these individuals were Peter's bosom buddies; no doubt some were his enemies. But it did mean that there was a great deal of *stability* to his relationships. He knew pretty much what to expect as he interacted with others, and they knew what to expect from him. This stability of relationships may have been boring at times, and Peter may have felt "stuck" with some pretty creepy folks (perhaps even a spouse of such description), but it did provide a sense of security. Peter knew that he could depend on those relationships during hard times (famine, disease, or death), and others knew that they could depend on Peter.

Martin Modern, on the other hand, is likely to live in a number of geographical communities during his lifetime. The requirements of education and occupation will most likely push him out of the nest and force him to become mobile. Not only that, but since his parents grew up within the constraints of modern mobility, it is likely that the home of his youth was actually the "homes" of his youth, and that he experienced the transitory life long before he extricated himself from the clutches of his parents.

What this implies is that Martin's relationships are of much shorter duration than Peter's were. It does not mean that they are less enjoyable or less pleasant, but they are, in general, less stable and shorter lasting. Martin must continually develop new relationships as well as terminate old ones. Relationships do not "fall" into his life as they did in Peter's. They are consciously chosen and cultivated, or else they do not exist. The last point is important. In Peter's world, choice was not a crucial factor to most relationships. They existed whether or not he wanted them. But, for Martin, when he moves to a new locale he *must choose* new friends or he will find himself without them. It is possible for Martin to be friendless in a way that Peter could not even imagine.

For Martin, moreover, there is a set of relationships that Peter rarely encountered. For the sake of short-hand, let us call them "functional relationships." They exist purely as a means to an end—as a way of getting something Martin thinks he needs. For example, when Martin goes shopping and picks up groceries, his relationship with the check-out clerk is a purely functional one. He has no intention or desire to develop a deep personal relationship with the clerk (unless their eyes meet and love blooms—another rather modern notion: instant love). He wants merely to purchase his eggs and vegetables, to carry on an exchange of valuables (currency for produce), and go on his way. The clerk, therefore, is a nonperson to him. The clerk's value to Martin is purely in the fact that he or she can perform the act of exchange. That is all.

Now the thing to notice is that many of Martin's relationships are of this kind. Follow Martin Modern through the day, and this point becomes obvious. From the time he leaves his home in the morning, the people he meets—the newsman, policeman, donut salesperson, elevator operator, and receptionist, not to mention the other drivers on the road—are pure functionaries to him. The same holds true for most of the relationships he encounters on the job. Indeed, it may very well be that the first nonfunctional relationship he will encounter is the one he has with his dog when he returns to his apartment at 5:30 that evening.

Thus we see that Martin has frequent contacts with other human beings, but a large number of them are not "dependable" in the sense that Peter's are "dependable." Many are relationships in which he has invested nothing personally, and they are meaningless to him as a person (though very helpful in a material sense). Let me put it bluntly: none of these relationships consist of people who care (more than theoretically) whether Martin Modern lives or dies. It is not that these people are hard-hearted (they may have hearts of gold); rather, the point is they do not have a caring relationship with Martin. Nor he with them.

There are clear advantages to Martin's relationships over Peter's, of course. The fact that he chooses them means that he has more discretion over the type of relationships he develops. Assuming he is good at this choosing process and others want to be chosen by him, he may create for himself a rather enjoyable constellation of friendships. He will not need to put up with boring companions nor feel trapped in unfulfilling relationships

Nevertheless, if Martin is not skilled at the choosing process, or if he is not considered a desirable person, he may rather quickly find himself alone. I mean really alone—with no one for him to depend on and no one to depend on him. The problem with the voluntary relationships of modern society is not that they are absent, but that they are distributed on the basis of demand rather than need.

TRADITION

Another significant change brought about by the modernization process relates to the role of tradition in everyday life. It is not an exaggeration to say that Peter Peasant was propelled through life by the inertia of tradition. Certainly, on a day-to-day basis, tradition defined his life for him. But even more important, it was tradition that shaped both the details and broad contours of his future. As a child, for example, Peter knew that his future occupation would, in all probability, be the same as his father's. Similarly, like everyone else in his family and community, he knew that his religious life would be dominated by a single religious institution. Tradition, moreover, handed him his values, his daily food intake, his marriage partner, and his lifestyle. In short, his future was significantly shaped by the past.

None of this means, of course, that Peter was some faceless automaton, programmed by tradition to make every decision. Nothing I have said should be construed to take the "humanness" out of Peter. He was still an active decision maker who was expected to make a large variety of choices. One important choice, for example, was whether or not to go along with tradition in every detail: Peter could exercise his right of veto ("I will not attend Mass this morning"), but he would have to pay a price ("No heathen like Peter will marry *my* daughter!"). Moreover, within the constraints of tradition, there were still a voluminous number of personal choices to be made. Shall I be tender, shabby, helpful, spiteful, energetic, lazy, charming, indignant, dastardly . . . ? The force of tradition did not obviate Peter's capacity to exercise a rich variety of human potential, but it required this exercise to be carried out within rather clear and precise boundaries.

Such a picture, however, contrasts sharply with the daily experiences of Martin Modern. For tradition tells Martin one thing and one thing only—that tomorrow will not be the same as today (i.e., that tradition is meaningless). It is a tradition of traditionlessness. Change—not tradition—is normal. Martin's daily experiences inform him that he must not rely on tradition, because tomorrow the traditions of today will be obsolete.

This is the case for a great number of reasons, certainly, but the rapid growth of technology must be considered a key factor. Mushrooming technological development tends to antiquate past procedures at an ever-increasing pace. What happens is that new techniques make past techniques "obsolete" by accomplishing tasks faster, or cheaper, or whatever. This makes those of us who possess "old" technology (last year's automobile or solar panels) feel as though we are not only behind in terms of style but also a bit irresponsible. By sticking with obsolete technologies, we are not "doing it" the best way it can be done.

Hidden under this cycle of technological change is a value—what I will call the *value of efficiency*. The reason we feel somewhat irresponsible when we hold onto old pieces of technology (a home without insulation or energy-saving equipment, for example) is that we have come to hold the value of efficiency in very high esteem. We believe it is irresponsible to do things inefficiently—to work harder than we need to work, to go around something when we can go through it, to waste heat when we can conserve it. Not only that, but we believe (sometimes wrongly) that efficiency is always less costly. Thus some of us buy a Mercedes Benz diesel automobile so that we can save money on maintenance and gasoline and thus make a "good investment." As a result, we often find ourselves spending gigantic sums of money in order to save money. One suspects, however, that the real motivation in such cases has something to do with possessing a thing of value and that the value of that thing is rooted in our appreciation of efficiency.

The consequences of living in a world of persistent change are substantial. Not only is tradition suddenly of little import, but "the moment" becomes absolutely crucial to our daily existence. The winner in life is the person who catches the moment, who perceives that now is the time to act if one wants to escape the obsolescence of yesterday. All of this suggests a very "now"-oriented individual, one who looks to the conditions of the present to make decisions about the future. David Riesman has called such individuals "other-directed" personalities because they look to others in order to decide how they should behave. We moderns are such people. Like overly sensitive mimics, we stretch out our antennae to receive all of the appropriate impulses and cues so that we won't be caught out of lock step with our contemporaries. *Relevance* becomes the salient word in our lives, for it is the key that opens up the doors to a suitable lifestyle, career, or mate. To be tuned in to the messages of the day is to be sociable and accepted. To be traditional is to be odd, or possibly even dangerous.

Surprising in this scenario is finding that the person who is most freed up from tradition, Martin Modern, is the one who is most captured by the social influences around him. When we think of Peter Peasant, we think of someone who was massively confronted by the power of social facts—the forces of tradition that limit his freedom as well as his opportunities. His life, to us, seems to have been abysmally constrained. But Martin is similarly constrained, not by heritage, but by the dictates of contemporary society. In a sense, he *chooses* to enslave himself to the shifting sands of modernity by depending on his immediate environment for feedback and direction.

The price of this choice is a significant loss of freedom. By focusing on that which changes, Martin assures himself of always being on the verge of antiquity—that is, of being out of date. To avoid that fate, therefore, he is forced to be ever more sensitive, ever more open, ever more receptive to the stimuli of his age. In short, in his escape from tradition, Martin Modern has become more—not less—sociologically predictable and conformist. One is tempted to say that the price of liberty from the traditions of the past is bondage to the fads of modernity.

VISION

There is a sense in which Peter Peasant lived in a world that was not of his own making. His world, as well as his place in that world, were "givens" to him. From his perspective, he did not determine his occupation (present or future), had little influence over the selection of a spouse, and was hardly in a position to choose his religious affiliation. Moreover, his social status within the community was more or less fixed at birth. Rare indeed was the person in Peter's village who would acquire an occupation different from that of his parents (unless it involved a move into the priesthood). Rarer still was the person who bettered himself by moving into an occupation of greater prestige. In such a society, status was not something to be earned but rather a fate that resulted from the way things were. Using the parlance of the sociologist, status was "ascribed" in Peter's world, not "achieved."

As a result, Peter's vision of the world was one that placed him in the context of forces larger than himself, forces that significantly shaped his environment and over which he had only marginal influence. This vision told Peter that his life was controlled by things that were awesome, fearful, and grand. God (or the gods), king(s), destiny, and tradition all played the role of agents that significantly constrained Peter's existence. These agents of control were things that Peter could either adapt to or resist, but they were clearly beyond his personal management. Thus his vision of himself in the world was one in which he is not the controller, but the objective of control.

To us modern types, such a vision seems extremely alienating. After all, if Peter *thinks* that his world is controlled by gods and traditions, then it *will* be controlled by gods and traditions—or, more accurately, by those who pose as the representatives of the gods (kings, magistrates, and the brokers of power). In effect, by giving in to the forces of history, hadn't Peter Peasant given up the possibility of changing his world for the better? In Marxian language, his "false consciousness" has left him vulnerable to the manipulation of the elites and thus incapable of changing his living conditions.

While it is true that Peter lived in a world of relative "helplessness" (from our perspective), one must not forget that he also existed in the context of relative security. And this was the bright side of Peter's existence normally left hidden from the modern eye. For while Peter may have felt powerless against the forces of fate, he also knew absolutely that he had a place in that fate. In other words, he knew that he was a part of something much bigger than himself, something that did not depend on him for its existence, but on which he could depend. His status in this life and the next was secure as long as he maintained certain minimal standards. What his vision lacked in puissance, it made up for in constancy, durability, and certitude.

Contrast again the situation of Martin Modern with that of Peter Peasant. Rather than being a world of "givens," Martin's world is one of "possibilities." It is a society whose ideologies suggest that status is not something to be inherited (unless, of course, one inherits a high status) but must be earned on the battlefield of life. Central to this conception of the world is the notion that life is what we make of it. One can be a president or a bum (or both), but we must be the masters of our fate. Neither the gods nor traditions must be our masters. They are the products of our imaginings, capable of controlling us only if we let them. The goal is to free ourselves of those things that constrain us—to shun those forces that box us in and keep us from expressing our *real* selves.

Above all, the modern vision is one of "choice." To refuse to choose is the height of irresponsibility, the deadliest of sins. Take marriage, for example. The modern ideal is to choose a spouse who is compatible with one's needs and personal preferences. Such a choice is made on the basis of a host of feelings and conceptions of bliss, but it is above all a choice made by the two individuals involved. Indeed, to suggest that anyone else ought to have anything at all to say about the selection of a spouse is to invoke the wrath not only of young lovers everywhere, but also of defenders of the constitution. The right to choose one's mate is fundamental.

Similarly, one has a responsibility to choose an occupation. To become a carpenter simply because one's parent was a carpenter is to shirk one's responsibility to oneself. At the very least, one ought to go out into the world, become exposed to the myriad of occupational possibilities, and try to match (by computer, if possible) one's personal gifts with the appropriate job. After that, if one still decides to become a carpenter, it will at least be a defensible choice.

Decisions of this kind ought also to be made in the realms of diet ("Am I getting enough fiber?"), family size ("Can I afford two children?"), friendships ("Will she fit into my clique?"), and exercise ("Morning, noon, or night?"). To refuse to make such choices is to abrogate one's responsibility to maintain control over one's world. It is to lose the modern vision.

This vision of choice, however, is a two-edged sword. Its primary advantage, obviously, is that it allows us to be—or at least think we can be—something different tomorrow from what we are today. It is (at least theoretically) a vision of hope, for it always insists that one can divorce oneself from the past in order to make a new future. And, in fact, the modern world is one that offers a range of opportunities far beyond anything that Peter Peasant could ever have imagined. Thus to the extent that one is talented, bright, and beautiful, the modern world offers a multiplicity of possibilities equal to the promises of the modern vision.

But in the midst of this "hope" the modern vision offers us, as well, the gift of *insecurity*. Why? Because

43

with the responsibility to choose comes the obligation of living with choices made. That is, the essence of choice is to make a decision between a number of alternatives, some of which are perceived as better than others. The possibility of choice, therefore, means that one also confronts the possibility of making poor choices—of "blowing it," to use the vernacular.

Peter Peasant, of course, was also subject to the possibility of making bad choices, but only within a limited range of activities, many of his choices having to do with moral and ethical matters. Martin Modern, however, not only confronts ethical decisions but also the responsibility to make decisions about education, occupation, locale, family, etc.—decisions that will dramatically affect his lifestyle in the years to come. This means that Martin must decide, as he studies math in eighth grade, whether or not he wants to become a physician when he grows up. If he fails to make the grade at that point, he must live with the vestiges of that failure for the rest of his life. And whether he blames that failure on genes, society, or self, he lives with the knowledge that things could have been different. It is a form of knowledge that was unknown to Peter and one that he rarely had to worry about. But Martin *must* worry. If he does not worry about his future, he will forfeit numerous opportunities. If he does not worry, he may fail.

It is true that, at times, modernity does offer Martin the possibility of a second chance. He can quit a job he does not enjoy and probably find another. He can divorce a wife he no longer loves and give another woman a whirl. He can drop his membership from the Congregational church and drop into the Episcopal parish across the street. But this rarely gives him the satisfaction he seeks, since his first go around on the job (or spouse, or whatever) must now be defined as a wasted opportunity.

More problematic than this, however, is the fact that starting over tends to undermine the meaning of the relationship in the first place. With each new divorce and wedding, for example, there is a necessary erosion of the meaning of the marriage bond itself. This will be true, despite the sincerity of the couple or their commitment to a traditional (till-death-do-us-part) arrangement, since the fact of divorce confronts them ipso facto with the possibility of choice. In other words, to move through a divorce confronts them with the knowledge that a marriage relationship is something over which they have power, not something that has power over them. Both its beginnings and its endings are under their control.

Ultimately, it is this power of the individual to control (at least theoretically) that becomes the major problem for the modern vision. To be in control is to be the source of one's future. To be in control is to declare one's autonomy from any higher authority. To be in control is to be (or play) god. While a great deal of power can accrue to those who hold such assumptions, there is an equivalent loss of meaning attendant on its acquisition. If I am the master of my fate, then life is what I can make of it—and nothing else. It means that norms and values and ethical systems have no more significance than the significance I can ascribe to them. It means that life itself is nothing more than the product of my imagination, to be used and abused as I see fit. It means (to juxtapose contradictory concepts) meaninglessness. Sociologists refer to it simply as anomie.

It is this logical flow within the modern vision— from choice to meaninglessness—that makes the events of the sixties and seventies understandable. To those (once called the older generation) who advocated "responsible choices," the flower children of the sixties were anathema. They stood for irresponsibility,

45

the pleasure of the moment, and ethical and social anarchy. But what should be clear is that the absurdities of these people had their ontological roots in the same modern vision that was so dear to the hearts of their parents. Step number one was taken when the first generation said (by deed more often than word) that we can make the world into our own image. Step number two was taken when the second generation responded, "Who cares?"

COMMUNITY

The relevance of this discussion to the topic of community is, I trust, self-evident. Community is *relationships*. It is a set of relationships that are durable, personal, dependable, and based on the inherent value of the community's inhabitants. Community is *tradition*. It is a pattern of life that is worthy—not because it is functional, or efficient, or reasonable—but simply because it has been cherished and handed down by previous generations. Community is also *vision*. It is a vision that assumes that the world is larger than self, that its meaning transcends the meaning I may give it, and that its significance comes from the One who created it, rather than from those for whom it was created. In other words, community is an unremitting coterie of relationships set within the context of specific traditions and rooted in a transcendent vision.

Such an understanding of community immediately reveals why it is that we modern types are perpetually on a quest for community without the slightest evidence that we ever attain it. Modernity fundamentally undermines the thing we seek. The forces of modernization require relationships that are instrumental and temporary, not durable and unremitting. The forces of modernization assume that activities must be rational and purposeful, not valued for their longevity and inherent meaning. The forces of modernization encourage a perspective that is autonomous and individuated, not dependent or transcendent. In short, the needs of community are significantly at odds with the requirements of modernity. And in the world of the West (the world in which a few of us reside and many others seek to emulate), the disputation between these two combatants has long since been resolved.

PART II / The Problem for Faith

three / **Modern Religion**

Up to this point I have argued that modern social conditions tend to undermine community. If that is true, then modernity's greatest impact ought to be felt in those areas of life where community is most essential. Two such areas, I believe, are the *family* and *religion*. In part III I will be exploring the impact of modernity on the family. Right now, however, let us take up the topic of religion. To what extent is religion a community phenomenon? And what effect has modernity had on the religious experience?

The Religious Community

Whatever else "being religious" may mean, most sociologists would agree that it involves community participation. Indeed, concerning the topic of religion, that may be the *only* thing on which they would agree. This is because, from a crosscultural perspective, it is relatively easy to discover religions that lack some of the other assumed "essentials." One can find, for example, religions that are devoid of beliefs about God or gods and totally lacking in any formal creedal propositions. But if one peruses the historical landscape of religious experience, one rarely discovers religions apart from a community—until, that is, today.

Relationships

The reason for the affinity between religion and community is apparent if we compare the basic elements of community with the needs of religion. First, it hardly requires saying that religion needs human relationships for its sustenance and vitality. But this need is not only for relationships in general but also for communal relationships in particular—those relationships rooted in dependability, longevity, and mutuality. Functional relationships, though necessary to the ongoing business of the religious organization, are not of primary importance. Personal relationships, on the other hand, are absolutely crucial.

One has only to think of some of the rites of religiosity to illustrate this point. What does it mean to offer or receive confession, for example? Is it to exchange personal values? Yes, in part. Confession can be personally satisfying, as can listening to the foibles of those who act like saints. But only a dolt would argue that such an exchange constitutes the confessional relationship. Foremost, confession assumes a mutual understanding of the human condition—not simply in the abstract, but existentially. It assumes that I am a wrongdoer (a sinner), for one thing. For another, it presupposes that I need to acknowledge that fact before others who are also wrongdoers and who also know the pain of unmitigated guilt. It is precisely because we share this insight that you and I have the capability of entering into such relationships. We understand each other's needs—deeply, personally, and fundamentally. That is what makes confession a viable human activity, and that is why, regardless of whether or not we are religious, we seek out other human beings to whom we can bare our souls.

Religious rites of passage also depend on communal relationships to attain their full significance. Confirmations, baptisms, weddings, and funerals are not simply hurdles that get the celebrants from one point to another, nor is their meaning confined to the religious function being performed. The reason for this is obvious: each of these rites is carried out for the community as much as for the individual(s) involved. This is obviously true in the case of a funeral, since, one assumes, the deceased acquires few benefits from the occasion. It is the bereaved family and friends who need the experience, and they will profit from it in direct proportion to the depths of the relationships they share with other members of the community.

Such is also the case, however, in those ceremonies in which participants are alive and kicking. The marriage ceremony, for example, is not only in and of itself a relational event; it exists for the community as well as for the couple. It is the community context, for example, that gives power to the wedding pledges, since the oaths made before God become matters of public record and are engraved on the community mind. The community is there to hold the couple accountable for the incredible things they have promised each another. Moreover, the power of the community at this point is dependent on the strength of the communal relationships, since the wedding couple is likely to feel less bound to pledges made in the context of nominal acquaintances. In other words, "till death do us part" is likely to be taken more seriously when promised in front of lifelong companions than in the presence of a bank teller, a Las Vegas minister, or empty pews.

Tradition

Religion, however, depends not only on the relationships of the community but also on its traditions. As carriers of meaning, traditions are important because they represent a taken-for-granted understanding of ultimate reality. That is, they are not things that need to be explained in detail every time they are invoked or exercised. Rather, we participate in religious traditions as if we understand their meaning (whether we do or not is another question) in part because those who have preceded us have also found them worthy and meaningful. In most cases then, traditions represent actions that precede thought. They exist to stimulate our hearts and minds along certain lines of thought (e.g., contemplating God's mercy or faithfulness), not for the purpose of debate.

The Lord's Supper, for example, is a Christian tradition in the strongest sense of that term. It is ancient and significant, drawing its power from the One who commanded it as well as gave it meaning. Thus when I participate in a communion service, I know that I am engaging in an activity binding me to Christians of all ages, from Peter to Mother Teresa, from Menno Simons to John Calvin. Moreover, as I eat the bread and drink the wine, my heart is skewered by the image of Christ, sacrificing Himself for me, shedding His blood to cover my impieties. In that moment, the tradition brings me face to face with my Redeemer, and

I am astounded by God's mercy, grace, and love. Such a moment is possible, however, only because I have taken the tradition as an assumption rather than a hypothesis. When I participate in the Lord's Supper, I am engaging in an act of appreciation, not a critical analysis. Indeed, to debate the theoretical arguments relative to the event is to miss the event altogether. Such debates have their place, to be sure, but not at the moment the tradition is being practiced.

Traditions, therefore, are important to the religious community because they remind the parishioner that not everything is up for grabs. They represent bulwarks of faith, beacons that remain undimmed in the tumultuous seas of everyday living. Although they are not the thing in which the community places its faith, they are the dependable moorings that link us to the objects of our devotion. The fact that they can be counted on—the fact that they can be assumed—is the thing that allows us to get on with the business of worshiping God. Adoration and praise do not emanate from the lips of those who are dissecting traditions but from those who are embracing them.

Vision

Finally, it should go without saying that the religious community must also have a transcendent vision. If ever there was a community rooted in the notion of a reality beyond itself, this most surely is the one. To be religious is to transcend oneself, to commune with a world larger than one's own world, to meet with a Power not of one's own making. Certainly, this ultimate vision does not always take the form of God (unfortunately, in my prejudiced opinion), but it does seek some kind of reconciliation with forces larger than the individual.

For the Christian, of course, this vision of transcendent reality is not at all a vague thing, though it is mysterious. Rather, it is the concrete reality of a God who creates, sustains, and relates to his creation. Fundamental to the Christian vision, therefore, is not only the belief that God exists, but that we are the products of his hands—that we are dependent on him for our existence. Thus our vision is not something we have concocted to suit ourselves, but a perspective that suits the Reality that has been communicated to us. Believing this, we have no choice but to make the vision central to the life of the Christian community.

THE PROBLEM OF VOLUNTARISM

What I have argued up to this point is simply that religion is a communal phenomenon. This in no way implies that individuals are irrelevant to questions of religiosity. Quite the contrary, individuals are the beings who experience religious phenomena. Nor does it suggest that religion is "just" community, for community is only the context of the experience and not the object of religious devotion. But it does mean that community—and its elements of relationships, traditions, and vision—is a core ingredient of the religious enterprise and that its absence over a period of time will seriously erode the vitality, if not the life, of the religious experience.

And that is precisely what has happened during the modern era. Even in the church, relationships, which are the bedrock of the religious community, are today often temporary. Traditions, which carry religious meanings from one generation to the next, are either nonexistent or stripped of their significance. And vision—that common understanding of both source and destiny—has been secularized beyond recognition. Before us, then, lies the question "Why?" Why has modernity played such havoc with the religious community?

One of the most significant factors in the interplay

of modernization and religiosity is the component of choice—let us call it the problem of voluntarism. Central to this problem is a very simple truth. As modernization progresses (or as it has progressed in the West), it increasingly transforms religious experience into a voluntary affair. By that I mean that the modern era, with its emphasis on individual decisions and choices, has turned religion into a matter of private discretion.

Remember again the life of Peter Peasant. This is an individual who was more than likely raised in a world of monolithic religiosity. His village was probably dominated by a single church organization that no doubt exercised considerable influence throughout the region. Peter's choices in the realm of faith, therefore, were relatively simple. He could move along the path of least resistance and become a full-fledged participant in the church; or, as an adult, he might try to simply ignore the church and live apart from it; or, more improbably, he might leave his community altogether and join a religious sect (possibly in hiding somewhere in the countryside).

Each choice had its consequences. The first option, participation, was clearly the easiest from a sociological point of view (though it may have been difficult to participate on a daily basis), since being a participant in the church was considered "the right thing to do." Despite its costs in time, money, and restrictions, it provided Peter with a sense of acceptance, well-being, and community citizenship (not to mention *eternal* citizenship). It was the route everyone was expected to take. The second option, avoidance, while freeing Peter from a variety of religious obligations, had the disadvantage of stigmatizing him. What it offered in personal freedom, it robbed him of in respect and social honor. The final option, flight, was the most difficult of all, since to choose another religious faith was to choose ostracism, excommunication, and possibly death. Conversion in Peter's world meant, quite literally, dying to one's past and living a radically altered future.

For Peter Peasant, then, religious choices were relatively few and clear-cut. Each option had its attendant problems and benefits, its merits and demerits. Most importantly, however, each option was absolutely clear in its consequences. Peter knew, as he made his decisions of faith, what the results of his choices would be, and he knew that many of these decisions were irrevocable. One did not merely saunter through life, choosing option three today, and two tomorrow. Every choice was consequential.

Martin Modern, on the other hand, exists in an ocean of religious choices. Indeed, he is presented with a veritable smorgasbord of religious options, from Roman to Orthodox, Lutheran to Brethren, Krishna to "get-rich-now," TM to EST. The menu from which he can choose is vast and diverse, his palate the object of everyone's interest. His world is a cacophony of religious sounds, each one clamoring for his ear. Alone, each musician may make beautiful music; but together, as an orchestra, these musicians are painful to the ear. Little wonder, then, that many Martins choose to absent themselves from the symphony altogether.

THE PROBLEM OF ASSOCIATION

The dissonance of religious pluralism, however, is not the real problem here. The central issue is the role that Martin Modern must play as an agent of selectivity. For not only does Martin have the option of choosing from a number of different religious alternatives, he is also *forced* to make such choices. His is a world, not of religious obligations, but of obligatory religious calculation. He is required routinely to evaluate his religious predilections.

Why is that? Why can't Martin live a life like Peter's? Why can't he simply accept the faith of his parents, appropriate it into his daily existence, and live a life of monolithic religiosity? Why is he obligated to choose? More to the point, can he not refuse to choose? Can't he live entombed in the religious world of his ancestors if he so desires?

No, he cannot. Regardless of how successful Martin's parents are at convincing him of the merits of their faith and regardless of how persuasive they may be about the truthfulness of its doctrines, Martin Modern will nevertheless be faced with the imperative of religious choice, called by Peter Berger the "heretical imperative" (in his book *The Heretical Imperative* [Garden City, N.Y.: Doubleday, 1979]). There are a variety of reasons for this imperative, not the least of which is the *problem of associations*. To be in the modern world is to associate with people who are different from oneself—to have friends with different hopes, dreams, diets, and doctrines. What this suggests is that, sooner or later, Martin will become friends with someone who believes quite differently from the way he does—someone whom he enjoys and respects, but who is nevertheless going to hell.

For a child, the first experience with the "problem of association" can cause a good deal of internal struggle and debate: "How can he believe that God doesn't exist? How can I believe that he does? How can we still be friends?" Such questions are so perplexing, in fact, that often they result in the termination of the friendship. But ending a friendship is only a temporary solution, for the problem will come up again and again, eventually leading to some kind of truce (i.e., agreeing to disagree) or a promise of indifference ("Let's just not talk about it"). In either case, such contacts force Martin to the following realizations: First, significant others (who are not stupid or vile) believe things he does not believe. And second, there are "reasons" for the beliefs of others, just as there are "reasons" for his own religious assumptions. For Peter Peasant, heretics were morons, or evildoers, or both. For Martin Modern, they are friends.

THE PROBLEM OF MOBILITY

A second factor in the requirement of choice is the *problem of mobility*—geographical and social. While the problem of associations is a matter of knowledge (i.e., the only reason Peter doesn't have to deal with it is that he does not have to face the fact that heretics are people, too), the problem of mobility is a matter of location. It stems from modern man's rather persistent inclination to move, not only from place to place, but also from position to position.

Compared with Peter Peasant, Martin Modern is a mobile mad man. While Peter is likely to live in one spot his entire life, Martin is apt to move three or four times in the first third of his life. If he is middle class, for example, he is likely to move at least once as a child, a second time to attend college, a third time to take his first job, and numerous other times in order to secure a promotion or another occupation. As a result, he finds himself thrown into a variety of different social contexts, each with its own peculiar life-styles, and each with its own definitions of social propriety.

On the surface, geographical mobility may appear to be the least problematic for the religious community. After all, one can usually find a similar church in one's new place of residence, possibly even within the same denomination. But the modern quagmire is not the result of a lack of religious alternatives, but of an overabundance of them. It would be relatively easy to move from town to town if each community had only one Christian church (assuming the person is a Christian). But in our era, one moves into a plethora of religious possibilities, not only within the Christian community, but often within specific denominations. The positive side of this equation is that no one is "stuck" with the only church in town. The negative side, however, is that the selection process itself evokes a whole new way of looking at church membership.

To search for a church is to engage in an evaluation. It involves a process of assessing the merits of a variety of different churches and choosing the parish that most effectively suits one's needs. I will discuss the consequences of this evaluation process a little later, but for now, suffice it to say that once Martin Modern has begun the church-search endeavor, he has left forever the world of Peter Peasant. He is now choosing his brand of religiosity.

Social mobility, by which we mean a move from one social environment to another (a promotion from the job of assembly line foreman to a managerial position is an example of upward social mobility) presents similar religious choices to the churchman. One of the clear patterns in American religiosity is the relationship between church affiliation and social class. Historically, this meant that certain denominations tended to have a preponderance of lower-class members while others catered to the upper class. Although this pattern has broken down somewhat, it is still substantially true that specific local churches are associated with particular types of people and that people from certain class backgrounds feel more comfortable in some churches than in others.

This suggests that a move from one social class to another will entail, if not the necessity of a church change, certainly the awareness of its desirability. Why? Because to remain in a blue-collar church after one has been promoted to a white-collar job, for example, is to live in a different world on Sunday than on week days. Moreover, joining a new church may actually help such an individual's career in that it will allow him to identify more fully with the white-collar world. Thus, a move to an upper-middle-class church might both reduce the dissonance of living in two different social worlds and increase one's chances of further advancement. Regardless of what such an individual may decide after pondering this matter, the mere exercise of pondering has plunged him pell-mell into the world of religious choices. For me to even contemplate the possibility that a new job may entail a church switch is to entertain the notion that my religiosity is a function of my occupational choices— heresy to Peter Peasant and, one suspects, to the Lord of the universe.

THE PROBLEM OF SOURCE

A third factor that imposes religious choices on Martin Modern is the media. This point is so obvious, and the media such objects of discussion, that we can give it short shrift. Aside from all the debates about the nature of the media's effect on politics and morality, one thing seems beyond dispute: the media are a major source of influence in the modern world. Television, the press, and the theater offer not only forms of diversion and entertainment, but also novel ways of thinking about a great variety of topics. And one of those topics is religion. Sometimes this subject comes under the rubric of science; at other times it is called education; once in a while it is even admitted to be religion. No matter. In each case, the media present their readers and listeners and viewers with an interpretation of the way the world operates and why. World views are communicated via the media.

As a result, anyone who holds a specific world view (Christian or otherwise) will of necessity encounter through the media perspectives that are antithetical to his own. Not periodically. Not in the context of debate. But persistently and without comment. This means that Martin Modern is daily faced with a barrage of information that runs counter to his specific religious beliefs (assuming that he has some—the easiest way to escape this torrent is to keep one's values nebulous and ill-defined). If nothing else, this forces Martin to realize that his creed is one among many, merely an option among a variety of possibilities.

Conclusion: The Problem of Vision

Finally, there is the modern vision itself, based as it is on the assumption of possibilities and the necessity of making a choice. When all is said and done, Martin Modern is not only confronted by religious voluntarism because he has friends whose beliefs differ from his, or because he moves from one social location to another, or because the media bombard him with religious options. He also makes choices about religiosity because his vision of the world informs him that it is his obligation to make such choices. That is, Martin is not only faced with the fact of having to make such decisions, but he also feels it is his responsibility to make them.

This is brought into clear relief by the question "Why?" If asked why he is a Presbyterian, Martin will not say it is because his parents were Presbyterians, or because he was raised in a Presbyterian community. Rather, he will jump into a frightfully long and detailed discussion of the merits and virtues of Presbyterianism. What is crucial, both to the one asking him this question and to Martin himself, is that the respondent has a rational defense of his religious membership. Indeed, if one is a truly modern questioner, Martin's ability to defend his Presbyterian identification will be far more important than the fact that he is a Presbyterian. In other words, of paramount importance is whether or not Martin has actually made a calculated decision to be a Presbyterian. If he has— if he can show that he has thought through the matter carefully and deliberately—then the fact that he is a Presbyterian is made legitimate. But if his answer is vague or confused, then we begin to suspect that Martin has not really considered the issue very carefully, or even worse, that he has not made a *decision* about his Presbyterianism at all (horrors!). And at that point we begin to doubt the veracity of his church affiliation altogether.

In any case, the crucial thing to us moderns is not that Martin is a Presbyterian, but that he has made a thoughtful decision about his church membership. In the modern vision, it is not what one believes that is important, but whether one can give a good account of why he believes it.

four / The Religion of Choice

Modernity creates a climate in which religious voluntarism is both necessary and, from the modern perspective, desirable. We live in a world that not only forces us to choose between a variety of religious beliefs and ultimate values but also informs us that it is in the choosing that we become better human beings. All in all, it is a rather convenient thing to have this vision of choice in the modern context, since choice itself is a matter of necessity. It is convenient but nevertheless costly—especially for the religious community.

SELLING RELIGIOUS AUTHORITY

To understand the effects of voluntarism on the religious community, we must not start with the community at all, but with the nature and transformation of religious authority. In the world of Peter Peasant, religious authority emanated from the authenticity of the religious institution itself. That is, the pronouncements of the church were authoritative because they came from the church. No other reason was needed. Sociologists would allege that the church had authority because it was "sacred" (something set apart from the everyday world of events and held in great awe and high esteem by the community). The reasons for its sacredness would be hotly debated by modern sociologists, but such a debate is perfectly irrelevant to our present discussion. The point simply is that the church—along with its traditions, edicts, and doctrines—spoke with the voice of authority. Its spokesmen did not "suggest" that the church's pronouncements were true, nor did they suggest that the parishioner ought to conform to them. They *were* true and binding. Peter Peasant could, of course, reject them, but that would mean that he would reject the church itself. What Peter did not do was openly choose from among them.

Such a picture of religious authority is totally alien to Martin Modern. For him, authority does not issue from the church, but resides within himself. He is the one who determines whether or not a belief is true, and he considers it his right and sworn duty to pick and choose from among the various possibilities. Authority, in Martin's world, is a purely subjective matter. It is a thing given by the subject (Martin) to the object (a church) for a limited duration of time and under a set number of conditions. As long as the religious institution performs according to the conditions prescribed by Martin, he may be willing to allow it a degree of authority in his life. But if it abrogates these agreements, or, more likely, if he decides that the conditions need to be changed, he can at any time withdraw his support and thereby annul the authority of the church. Thus, religious authority in the modern context is relative to the whims of the parishioner. From the perspective of Peter Peasant, it would not appear to be authority at all.

Now, the fact that religious authority is dependent on the capriciousness of the layman means that the religious community, rather than imposing its will on individual members, must market it instead. That is, modern religious organizations are confronted with the task—the very important task—of selling their authority on the open market of religiosity. As Peter Berger has shown, the market analogy is an apt one in the modern context. The premise of modernity is that people consume religious ideas as they do potato chips and Coke. They live in the midst of a variety of different religious groups, each one offering something a little different to entice the customer.

Martin Modern, moreover, assumes that it is his obligation to be a religious consumer. When Martin moves into a new community, for example, it is commonly assumed that he will want to "shop around" for a new church—to sample all the various and sundry delicacies before sitting down for the main course. Even after he has decided to adopt a particular parish, however, the evaluation process continues. Especially during the first few months of his stay, the church is clearly on probation. Will Martin like the music? What will he think of the Sunday-school program? Does he enjoy an expository sermon or would he prefer a theme-beam approach? Are the people friendly enough (without being too friendly)? Will he feel comfortable with the morning worship service? These are just a few of the questions asked of the church on probation. It is Martin's answers to these questions that will determine whether or not he stays—whether or not, that is, he makes a substantial investment in the church.

On the surface, market religiosity may seem a fairly innocuous thing. After all, what harm can there be in a church trying to please its customers? On further investigation, however, the picture becomes less serene. There is, for one thing, the problem of assessment. How does a church know whether or not it is doing a good job? On what basis does a church evaluate its "success"? For the church of Peter Peasant, that question would have been very difficult to answer (and would probably never have been asked). There was simply too much going on in the local parish (too many functions, rituals, and responsibilities) to make a determination as to what constituted success.

THE GOD OF GROWTH

Not so for the church of Martin Modern's day. In a market environment, success means one thing and one thing only—customers. The number of consumers is the key criterion of a successful business, and "numbers" are the chief indicator of a successful modern church. A good church is a growing church. A dynamic assembly is one that is bringing in new recruits and filling up the pews. A dead church, on the other hand, is a church with shrinking attendance. Ask a stranger or two (at a religious convention, for example) to evaluate their home church, and most of the time they will initiate their response with a statement about growth. It is the quintessential barometer of the successful twentieth-century religious organization.

The impact of this emphasis on growth can be readily discerned in the modern conception of a successful pastor. If the health of a religious organization is determined by the number of new recruits, then the successful minister will be the one who is able to attract the most customers. Thus we discover that the most important quality a pastor can have is salesmanship (euphemistically described as one who is Spirit-filled, dynamic, charismatic, inspiring, powerful, etc.). The crucial questions are these: Is he a good speaker? Does he have a winsome personality? Will he be able to "preach the Word" effectively (i.e., "sell the church")? These are the questions of the modern pulpit committee, and these are the questions that are determining the type of pastors hired in the modern church. Never mind they are unrelated to 90 percent of what a pastor does (or ought to do). Never mind that they have no bearing on the depth of a pastor's affection for his flock. Never mind that they completely bypass questions about spiritual discernment, or love of neighbor, or love of God. Never mind these issues. The paramount issue remains. Can he recruit?

Another consequence of this passion for growth is a heightened sense of competition among churches. If we return to the market analogy, this phenomenon is not difficult to comprehend. Competition, of course, is a fundamental condition of the market. Businesses—or, in this case, churches—compete with one another for customers. In bald form, what this means is that one church's increase in attendance is another's demise. Social scientists call this kind of situation a zero-sum game. Theoretically, of course, religious organizations do *not* operate in a zero-sum atmosphere, since there is always a large number of people who attend no church at all; these folks represent a large untapped "customer pool" for any religious group seeking to grow. In real life, however, the data suggest that most Christian churches (including evangelical churches) do not grow by attracting the unchurched, but by enticing dissatisfied customers from other churches. These people are in no sense converts. Rather, they are merely "switchers" looking for the most comfortable and enjoyable place to worship. In the real world, therefore, it *is* a zero-sum game, and most church leaders are astutely aware of that fact.

THE GOD OF EFFICIENCY

One of the consequences of competition is a heightened interest in efficiency. Obviously, if a business is to compete successfully in a market, it is to its advantage to be as efficient as possible. Churches, like other businesses, therefore, attempt to cultivate those activities that are cost-effective and cull out those that produce the fewest "results." The question is: How does a church determine which activities are the most efficient? The answer, quite clearly, is to be found in evaluating the results of an activity in relation to the objectives of the institution. The key question, then, becomes: Does an activity bring about the desired outcome at minimum cost? Crucial to this question is one's definition of "desired outcome," since that will be the measuring rod against which all activities will be evaluated. And what is the desired outcome of the modern church? That question has already been answered: growth.

This burning desire for efficiency is problematic for the religious community, however, because most of the relationships in a traditional community are either irrelevant to, or contradict the value of, efficiency (defined in terms of growth). Take the relationships of the pastor once again. The pastor is someone who is normally expected to care for the people of the church. Caring means establishing long-term relationships with parishioners so that he can understand their needs—not just as they say they exist in a couple of counseling sessions, but as he knows these needs from day-to-day contact. It is this relationship that ought to provide the pastor with the wealth of information he needs as he seeks to comfort and challenge, encourage and rebuke, console and prod. It is in knowing his flock that a preacher becomes a pastor. It is out of the depths of these relationships that he learns how to serve.

But the modern pastor has little time for such relationships. Indeed, they are palpably inefficient activities because they interfere with his primary task of recruitment. It is the Sunday-morning message that must take precedence over relationships, because the sermon is clearly the main attraction. People come to hear the pastor, not relate to him. Store hours are from 9:00 to 12:00 every Sunday morning. That is when the customers do their shopping and that is when the pastor must be in top form. Oh, sure, we want the pastor to have friends, and we certainly expect him to know our names as we parade out the front door. But, most of all, we want him to give us a stunning sermon on Sunday morning. If he cannot do that, he has obviously missed his calling.

The impact of efficiency, however, goes far beyond the relationships of the pastor. The modern church attempts to structure many of its relationships in order to provide for "an effective delivery of services." This noble goal is pursued primarily through the establishment of offices or positions, each of which is designed to meet specific needs within the church. For example, positions are created not only to oversee general areas of concern (evangelism, missions, education, etc.) but also to handle the details of every conceivable eventuality—details ranging from nose-wiping responsibilities to homiletics instruction. Indeed, one of the primary tasks of a person occupying a position in the modern church is to create additional positions under his or her area of responsibility so that those positions can in turn create more positions.

All of this, of course, is necessary to gain efficiency

and "deliver needed services." It is no wonder, then, that in some churches today there are actually more positions on paper than there are church members to fill them. Not to worry. As long as the church keeps growing, someone will be found to fill the vacancies (and create more vacancies). If all of this sounds familiar, there is good reason. The above description of a modern church is also an apt description of a bureaucracy—and this is precisely what the overevaluation of efficiency leads to, regardless of the type of organization involved. The modern church is, quite simply, one more contemporary institution in hot pursuit of bureaucratized relationships.

THE PROBLEM OF RELIGIOUS BUREAUCRACY

For those readers who find themselves nonplused by this analysis, let me quickly add that there is nothing inherently evil about a bureaucracy, just as there is nothing inherently wrong with the desire for efficiency. Similarly, a church cannot be faulted for wanting to deliver its services in the most effective manner possible. However, when this desire is the primary desire of the society at large and when the singular objective of the church is to ape social forces, then the pursuit of efficiency is extremely dangerous, especially to the community itself. Let us see why.

The first problem is that as we create positions in the church, we also create specialists to fill them. Each of these specialists (we hope) is especially gifted and/or trained to accomplish particular tasks. What this means, however, is that we become increasingly willing to let these specialists do the jobs that community relationships were originally intended to accomplish (e.g., sharing grief, comforting those with personal problems, giving financial assistance, and providing godly wisdom). Not only do these specialists bypass and undermine community responsibility, but they also perform their tasks in the context of a "functional" relationship. They dispense a service or perform a task, but they do not offer (in fact, they cannot offer) a long-term relationship. As a result, modern parishioners are neither taught by people who are familiar with their needs nor counseled by those knowledgeable of their situation, nor are they truly comforted by anyone. In short, just as in the society at large, personal relationships within the religious community have increasingly become supplanted by professional, functional relationships.

A second problem with the value of efficiency relates to its impact on church traditions. As was said earlier, traditions are important to the religious community because they represent taken-for-granted understandings of reality. Their power comes not from what they are, but what they symbolize; their purpose is not to provoke debate, but understanding. The problem, however, is that the value of efficiency directly contradicts the value of tradition. Efficiency evaluates; tradition accepts. Efficiency asks if there is a better way; tradition knows no other way. Efficiency means change; traditions are timeless. Although this list could continue, the point ought to be obvious: the purposes of these two values are substantially at odds with each other.

Now, one might argue that as long as the values of efficiency (or bureaucracy) and tradition coexist, they will perform the role of checking each other's eccentricities. But if either value becomes predominant, serious problems arise. Peter Peasant, as one might imagine, lived in a time when tradition was king; he and his religious community, therefore, no doubt suffered at the hands of unbridled traditionalism. We modern types, however, live in an era when traditions are meaningless and efficiency is all-powerful. Hence, today even the religious community seems incapable of warding off the eccentricities of efficiency ·or the concomitant demise of religious traditions.

One indication of this fact is the modern compulsion to question religious ritual. Indeed, at times it appears that no one in the modern church is able to engage in any Christian rite without apologizing for it or questioning its value altogether. While questions do need to be asked of traditions periodically, the persistent asking undermines completely the purpose of the tradition. Instead of provoking the religious celebrant to linger over the thing symbolized, questions of efficiency are capable only of provoking a discussion of the symbol itself. In fact, the modern church · spends far more time evaluating its traditions (for things such as authenticity and historicity) than it does learning from them. The end result of this march down Efficiency Lane is either traditions without significance or churches without traditions. In either case, the church becomes a church without community.

A Change in Vision

Most problematic of all, however, may be the impact of the spirit of efficiency on the vision of the religious community. To understand this adequately, however, we will need to ruminate momentarily on a finding of German sociologist Max Weber. In his study of social organization, Weber came to an interesting conclusion about the growth of the modern bureaucracy. A rough paraphrase of his conclusions is that as bureaucracies mushroom in size, they become increasingly consumed with the matter of their own survival and decreasingly concerned with the matters that gave them birth. Thus, a hospital becomes more concerned about surviving as a hospital than it does about the survival of its patients, a government becomes more concerned with the perpetuation of its existence than the dispensation of needed services, and a church invests an

ever-larger percentage of its budget into the maintenance of the church bureaucracy.

For the church, however, the ramifications of this
process go far beyond a shift in the church budget.
This is because the move from traditional goals to
survival goals entails a complete change in the purpose of the religious community—it is literally a
change in vision.

Means

Organizationally, this shift in vision results in an
increasing concern with "means" over "ends." The important question of the modern church is not, What
shall we do? but, How shall we do it? How can we
get more Sunday-school space? How can we make the
morning service more entertaining? How can we get X
to do Y? How can we keep X from doing Z? This
shift, of course, is not surprising in a technological
age. We moderns are far more confident of our ability
to deal with "how" questions than with "what" questions. Nevertheless, this fixation on means crowds out
questions of ends and, in the long run, the means
themselves become our ends. Thus, our "purpose" as
a church is to grow and prosper, and the driving
question for the church leadership is, How can we
accomplish those objectives? One should note, however, that in asking this question the church is searching for means to accomplish other means, not means
to accomplish an end. The means themselves have become our vision.

Relevance

This emphasis on the means of survival has also had
a significant effect on the development of the religious
community's theological vision. To survive in a market, a church must not only sell itself as a desirable
commodity; it must also sell its theology. Its beliefs

75

and biblical interpretations need to be convincingly presented to the consumer (or the consumer won't buy, and the church won't survive). In such an environment, it becomes extremely difficult to sustain a traditional, unchanging church dogma. The pressures to modify and transform church dogma in order to adapt to the needs of the customer are immense. "Relevance," not tradition or medieval church councils, becomes the primary criterion for good theology.

Thus the modern pastor seeks to relate his theology to all the major issues of the day, from pop rock to polyurethane, from sexual preference to social deference. This relating process, however, is not simply an effort at connecting religious dogma with everyday life (a laudable goal, certainly). Rather, it has become an attempt to make beliefs relevant to whatever Martin Modern determines to be his most pressing needs. In other words, the starting point in such theological discussions are the perceived needs of modern man. When such is the point of departure, an altered vision cannot be far down the road.

It is important to note, moreover, that the problem of theological relevance is not just a "liberal problem" or a problem attendant only on the liberal church. Although conservative Christians are adept at discovering perverted theologies among their liberal brethren, evangelicals are also victims of this tendency. Not only do they select theological positions that tend to support the political status quo, but they are also quite good at concocting theological remedies for personal ills. Indeed, I would argue that the success of the evangelical church in the last ten years is due, at least in part, to its ability to develop theological positions that suit the needs of the modern middle- and lower-middle-class consumer (for security, stability, and material justification). In some cases, the problem is not so much that these positions are wrong, but that they are incomplete and one-sided. Such skewed theologies are dangerous, however, not only because they neglect much of what is important in the traditional Christian message, but because they too are rooted in a consumer mentality. They are heard because they succeed; they succeed because they sell; and they sell because they contain ingredients that are considered desirable by the consumer. It is a vision designed to satisfy the customer.

CONCLUSION: A MODERN TRAGEDY

In the long run, of course, such consumer-based visions (conservative or liberal) are self-defeating precisely because they are based on the presuppositions of modernity. By developing theological principles around the interests of the customer, the church ensures itself of eventual obsolescence and/or irrelevance. What is fashionable to the consumer today will be obsolete tomorrow. The church with a fashionable vision in one era is destined for obscurity in the next.

It is possible, of course, for the church to avoid this eventuality by modifying its vision with the changing tide of popular opinion. But over time such an approach tends to undermine the reason most people are attracted to the church in the first place. If the church cannot offer an eternal perspective, of what value is it? If the church's vision is as flexible as the ideologies of modernity, how can the customers find any lasting solace there?

The answer is simple. They cannot. And thus the ultimate irony of the contemporary church vision is that in its attempt to be relevant, it renders itself singularly useless and ultimately irrelevant. The tragedy, however, is that in its headlong rush into oblivion, the religious community is vanishing as well.

PART III / The Problem for Family

five / The Family of Choice

I began the discussion of modern religion with the argument that religion is a communal phenomenon in need of all the elements of community to function properly. I started with this assertion, not only because I believe it to be true, but because many in the modern world fail to appreciate—or even acknowledge—religion's communal characteristics.

In regard to the *family*, however, I need make no such argument. Family, by common consent, is a communal affair. One may debate whether or not it contains all the elements of community; in the modern context, for example, some would question the neces-

sity for family traditions. But not many would argue
whether or not the family entails relationships. The
family *is* a set of relationships. An individual, on the
other hand, is *not* a family, and we would think it
nonsensical for one to be considered such.

We will begin our exploration of the modern family,
then, not with an argument, but with a story. It is a
tale that is not only true, but also illustrative of the
state of the modern family.

A Modern Odyssey

I know of a man who has by all accounts lived a
charmed life. From an early age, he seemed to exhibit
all the attributes we associate with success. He is in-
telligent and has always excelled in academic pursuits.
He has a warm, engaging personality and is a person
to whom others are naturally drawn. To this list one
could add that he is a good athlete (an outstanding
high-school basketball player), a reasonably good musician, and a nice-looking chap. Although he is certainly
not without his faults, one might say that, all in all,
he is an exemplary human specimen.

Sometime during college, he decided that he wanted
to attend seminary following graduation, with the hope
of one day becoming a full-time member of the clergy.
This surprised no one, since he had always been an
active church member and a thoroughly committed
Christian. Besides, he seemed to fit the image of an
ideal pastor. Outgoing and friendly, he managed to
combine the qualities of an extrovert with those of a
wise counselor. It was easy to envision him as a pastor, both in and out of the pulpit.

After college, for the next fourteen years or so,
things continued to go well. He married his high-
school sweetheart, graduated from a prestigious seminary, and assumed the pastorate of a struggling non-
denominational community church on the outskirts of a

major American city. Within five years, the church grew from 150 members to almost 500; in another five, the church was holding three services every Sunday in a sanctuary that held over a thousand parishioners. In the modern sense of the word, he was clearly a "successful" minister.

As a father and husband he was also a "success." Better than that, he was a genuinely devoted father and loving husband. If you asked any one of his five children, they would tell you that they had the greatest dad in the world. A similar question relative to his role as husband would probably have evoked the same response from his wife. Indeed, by all accounts, he was an outstanding family man. By his actions, it was apparent that he valued his family more highly than his job—a difficult thing for a "successful" pastor to accomplish.

And yet, only a few days before his fifteenth wedding anniversary, this same man was willing to set aside the roles of father, husband, and pastor in order to assume the status of lover. Putting it in the vernacular, he ran off with another woman.

FAMILIAL VOLUNTARISM

How could a man of such accomplishment do such a thing? This question has frequently been asked during the past few years because the man in this story is not unique. Many people in all walks of life have chosen to repudiate their past in the hope of redesigning their future. What is intriguing about these ventures is that they are not the product of failure. They do not occur because people are trying to extricate themselves from calamities. Rather, they happen in spite of success. Even the best of circumstances (modernly defined) seem powerless to prevent them.

Such events in the lives of the successful are usually attributed to a "mid-life crisis"—assuming, of

83

course, that they happen during mid-life—and I have no wish to quibble with that designation. But it is important to understand that events of this kind are not simply the result of aging bodies or youthful fantasies. They happen because we live in a society that renders them not only possible but, I would argue, probable. The social conditions of modernity are highly seductive; they are the lure, and we are the catch. And the fishing has been very good.

To understand why this is the case, one needs only to recall that the essence of modernity is choice. Its fundamental impact on the family, therefore—like its effect on religion—is to make familial relationships and traditions subject to a wholly voluntary vision. That is, it reduces the family to a matter of predilection. Take marriage, for example.

MARRIAGE

For Peter Peasant, marriage was a relatively straightforward event, judged by modern standards. For one thing, the selection of a spouse was primarily a parental responsibility. This does not mean that the young people had no say in the matter, since they were often able to influence the final outcome through informal channels. But the decision itself was made by the parents. As a result, mate selection was not based exclusively on mutual infatuation, but it also included some assessment of the perceived needs of the family. (Such an assessment, of course, was by no means made purely on altruistic grounds; parents calculated their own needs in making the decision.)

This parental "choice," however, was not unconstrained. A mate had to be selected from within certain religious, economic, and ethnic groups ("rules of endogamy") and outside of others ("rules of exogamy," usually pertaining to kinship and sex groups). Moreover, a large variety of unique traditions most likely delimited the final choice, depending on the culture in which it took place. In short, even the parents' decision regarding their child's marriage partner was a rather restricted one, subject to the constraints of tradition.

Today, of course, such a rigid approach to marriage is out of the question. We moderns want options, not constraints, and we have designed the family accordingly. Our choices, however, begin, not with the selection of a spouse, but with the idea of marriage itself. It is not simply a smorgasbord of partners that confronts us. It is a vast array of marital hypotheses.

To begin, the institution of marriage is a questionable commodity. Within the modern context, its value and necessity is not altogether apparent. For Peter Peasant, the value of marriage was beyond dispute: it provided material as well as social security. To us, however, marriage is merely one social arrangement among many. Its value to us personally, therefore, hinges on whether or not we find it convenient and potentially fulfilling.

Now note what this means. Both Peter Peasant and Martin Modern may ask the question, "Should I get married?" but by it each means something entirely different. For Peter Peasant this is a question (1) that implies a decision (which he will not make alone, remember) about something assumed to be valuable and (2) the answer to which will have significant consequences for his future. Peter Peasant, for example, may decide to remain celibate; perhaps he wants to become a member of the clergy. That decision, however, is not made because marriage is valueless, but despite the fact that marriage is greatly esteemed. Moreover, Peter's decision not to marry will mean that he will give up a certain way of life, including (ideally, at least) the possibility of sexual fulfillment as well as having children. For Peter Peasant, then, it is a highly consequential decision.

When Martin Modern asks, "Should I get married?" he means something entirely different. For him it is a question about both the value of marriage and its value to him personally. Thus he asks whether the institution of marriage is the best way for him to satisfy his needs. If it is, fine; if not, he can discover other avenues to fulfillment. Note, however, that regardless of how Martin Modern answers that question, his answer will not (compared with Peter Peasant's answer) profoundly change his life (unless he so chooses). To be blunt, in modern society Martin may reject marriage but live, sleep, and reproduce with the women of his (and their) choice.

None of this means that Martin necessarily enjoys marriage less than Peter, or that marriage is less appealing in Martin's society. Indeed, marriage may actually be more popular in modern societies. But popularity must not be confused with value. Most moderns continue to choose marriage, not because of the inherent value of the institution, but because it is still the option we assume will bring us the greatest happiness. In other words, its value is based solely on its ability to please. If it fails to deliver on that promise, we moderns are quite willing to jettison it.

COURTSHIP

For the modern individual who chooses to get married, the marriage-value decision is only the first of many. For one thing, there is the question of a spouse. To whom should one get married? That is an amusing query only to those moderns who have never asked it. To everyone else, it elicits reactions ranging from a mild case of nerves to fits of uncontrollable nausea. Such reactions are not difficult to understand. The selection of a spouse is all too often a modern horror story.

Keeping in mind the relative ease through which

Peter Peasant obtains a spouse, let us ruminate on the modern courting predicament. First, there is the problem of rules. On the one hand, by casual observation, one would conclude that there are no rules whatsoever restricting mate selection in modern societies. People form unions that seem to mix every conceivable religion, class, tribe, or sex. Indeed, at times it appears that any kind of person will suffice. On the other hand, as those who go through the search process well know, appearances can be quite deceiving. In point of fact, there is a great deal of informal pressure to select a mate with certain economic, educational, racial, and creedal credentials. Because these rules are seldom spelled out clearly, however, they remain a constant source of irritation to the marriage candidate. Under such conditions, one is tempted simply to ignore them altogether (to do this, remember, is a genuine possibility in modernity).

The problem of rules exists, in part, because there is also some confusion about who actually selects the spouse. Theoretically, of course, there is no confusion: I select my own spouse. That is one of the foundational principles of modernity. In reality, however, a whole cadre of people try to shape one's decision. Parents, pastors, pals, and potentials all attempt to coax one toward certain options and away from others. In the modern context, this sideline coaching can be infuriating precisely because the marriage decision is "none of their business." All of these friendly advisers, therefore, are an "interference" because they have no legitimate right of involvement. Moreover, should my spouse selection turn out to be a bad one, none of these willing advisers is about to take responsibility for my mistake. Little wonder, then, that they are considered more of an irritation than a help.

In addition to the complexities of rules and responsibility, there is also the problem of "tingle." The modern marriage candidate must not only be in accord with ill-defined rules and irresponsible advice, he or she must also elicit the all-important "tingle"—that feeling, euphemistically called love, which portends eternal bliss. This presents a problem, of course, since not that many people make us tingle. Assuming we fail to arouse tingles in others in proportion to their failure to arouse us, one perceives the modern courting predicament. It is a picture of millions of adult men and women, caught between modern myth and reality, on a quest for the mutual tingle.

GOVERNANCE

For those modern couples who arrive at the altar—assuming the use of that archaic artifact—choice remains an ever-present vexation. Indeed, in contrasting the worlds of Peter Peasant and Martin Modern, it is a far more significant issue during marriage than courtship. After all, both Peter and Martin are faced with the need to make premarital choices, albeit choices significantly different in kind and degree. After the wedding, however, Peter's familial decisions decrease markedly. Martin Modern's, on the other hand, have only just begun.

There is, in the first place, the question of governance. What kind of marriage relationship is to be established? In the modern context, there is a plethora of possibilities. There is the "traditional" patriarchal arrangement (sexist Model A) wherein the husband is the assumed seat of authority. A second possibility is a matriarchal arrangement in which the wife is the primary decision maker (sexist Model B). The democratic approach is another modern alternative, one that attempts an even distribution of authority between husband and wife. This model may or may not be extended to incorporate children. Still other models are conceivable, depending on the age of the children and the number of parents. No matter. The point is merely that modern marriage partners must *decide* how to relate to each other.

The freedom to decide is a grand thing, of course, assuming that one is confident about which option is preferable and assuming, too, that one's mate has made the same choice. Unfortunately, this is often not the case. Some governance models work better under certain circumstances (social, psychological, etc.) and worse under others. For this reason, many modern family counselors suggest that we attempt to match the model with the circumstance, selecting the best governance structure for each situation. Alas, if only humanity would fall in line with the therapists' advice. Instead, we find that circumstances change much too quickly to be neatly stuffed into the straitjacket of one particular model. One model may work successfully when Sally steals a cookie from the cookie jar; it may be less effective, however, when Johnny urinates in Dad's favorite loafers. To make swift rational moves from model to model, depending on the circumstances, is a bit much to ask even of the most modern parent.

The bottom line is that human beings are not capable of adopting the ideal model in every situation. Finitude and the Fall make that quite impossible. Modern people, however, failing to understand this, and driven by the need to make choices, find themselves on a perpetual search for the ideal governance model. And in so doing, they end up undermining the purpose of the model itself.

This can be readily understood if we translate "model" into "tradition." Family governance models are nothing more than modern conceptions of family traditions. Indeed, most of the models from which we moderns choose are the traditions of another (past or present) culture. The difference between moderns and traditionalists, however, is that we moderns attempt to select our models from an array of cultural traditions (in order to find the ideal), while the traditionalists simply take their models (i.e., traditions) for granted. What this means is that we moderns attempt to use traditions to suit our needs. The value of a tradition, however, is that it obviates the need for a decision. It allows us to get on with life without worrying about the details (of who does what and when). The question is, "How can one consciously use a tradition and take it for granted at the same time?" More difficult still, how can one constantly shift from one tradition (model) to another, and take each for granted in the process? Of the first possibility, I am skeptical; for the second, I see no hope.

RESIDENCE

The modern marriage is also confronted with the question of residence: Where shall we live? The residential issue itself, of course, is not new. When two people become one (assuming monogamy for the moment and ruling out the possibility of incest), the laws of physics suggest that at least one of the marriage partners must move. In most premodern societies, this matter was clearly spelled out. Newlyweds would either move in with the wife's family (matrilocal), the husband's family (patrilocal), or possibly establish a new place of residence (neolocal), usually close to one or both of their parents. Whatever the pattern, the exact nature of the move was clearly understood by the engaged couple long before the wedding day. It was explicitly defined by custom and tradition.

The modern couple operates under a neolocal pattern. This means that they can choose where they wish to live, so long as it isn't with the parents of either of them. They are free, theoretically, to decide the residency issue for themselves. This freedom is theoretical because, as every married couple knows, a great variety of social, psychological, and economic factors constrain this "free" decision. In reality, this couple is free from an extended-family tradition only, not from social forces.

The residency question, however, is not a single question but many questions wrapped into one. In order to decide where to live, the married couple—being two people rather than one—must first determine who will make the decision. Husband? Wife? Children? Parents? A general plebiscite? The possibilities are endless because custom provides no definitive answer.

A more crucial question, possibly, is what factors will determine the decision. That is, on what values or perceived needs will the residency issue be resolved? Having few traditions to fall back on, many modern couples allow economic factors to determine the location of their first home. The question, then, is not really, "Where shall we live?" but, "Where can I find the best job?" That question opens a Pandora's box, not only because "best job" is a nebulous category (unless, of course, one is willing to define it purely in financial terms), but also because there are normally two I's in the marketplace. Both husband and wife are looking for the "best job." To find a location that meets the vocational needs of both spouses is a monumental undertaking—so much so that some couples spend years in search of the residential ideal where both spouses can find job fulfillment.

It is no wonder, then, that couples who discover a community that provides mutual job satisfaction feel extremely fortunate. And yet, as difficult as it is to discover such an ideal, it may be only a Pyrrhic victory. Why? Because the ideal of mutual job fulfillment neglects so many other important considerations. What about the needs of children for good schools and

91

neighborhoods? What about the desire for a pleasant environment (near beaches, mountains, or lakes) and good weather? What about the need for cultural outlets, entertainment, and recreation? The list is endless. And its fulfillment unattainable.

Interestingly, such a list—because it is a modern catalog—does not even raise questions about relationships. And so in this list we see nothing at all about parents, grandparents, or special friends. After all, who would choose a home just to be near such as these? Not the modern couple! There are too many other more important decisions to make.

SEXUALITY

In the modern marriage, there is another question of no small significance. What sort of sex life do we wish to have? Once again, we are confronted with a very new question about the most ancient of activities. Sexual intercourse has been around for some time. Indeed, every human being is a living testimonial to its timeless popularity. What is new about human sexuality is our propensity, not to act, but to discuss ad nauseam the technical details.

On this point I wish not to be misunderstood. I am not comparing our society unfavorably with some prudish, sexually stifling regime. Nor am I arguing that modern society is the only one openly flaunting sexual liberation. The libido has been thoroughly celebrated throughout the ages, at times with great gusto and artistic panache. What separates us from the ancients, however, is our willingness to shift the emphasis from the goal of sexual fulfillment to the means of sexual gratification.

The modern couple is confronted with a panoply of sexual possibilities. These possibilities are presented as avenues to sexual enjoyment and are intended to prevent boredom, routine, or failure. Especially failure.

Few things are more dreadful in our era than sexual bankruptcy. And so, to prevent such a debacle, the modern couple is obligated not only to talk about sexual matters, but to read no fewer than a hundred sex manuals describing every conceivable conjugal activity. The aim of this educational process is to acquaint the couple with a plethora of sexual options, after which they can choose those techniques that most appropriately conform to their needs and desires. Once this is accomplished, there is the promise of sex that never sours.

The advantages of modern sexuality are obvious. Theoretically, at least, no one is stuck with techniques that never satisfy or routines that never fulfill. The problem, however, is that sexual enjoyment is a relative matter—relative both to past experience and to future expectations. There is no point at which one can say with authority that he or she has reached the pinnacle of sexual fulfillment. There is always the possibility of a "better" experience. Moreover, because our society exudes sexual fantasy, modern men and women are confronted daily with depictions of supremely satisfying sexual relationships—on television, at the theater, and in most popular literature—relationships they cannot possibly emulate but about which they can nevertheless dream. As a result, modern definitions of sexual satisfaction are often unrealizable.

The modern couple, therefore, is faced with a deadly combination: unreachable sexual goals and unlimited sexual options. Always under the assumption that a better sexual experience is possible, we moderns are on a perennial hunt for new techniques and superior methodologies. As a result, we discover option after option, each one heralded as a hedonistic savior, but each one failing to live up to its billing. Unfortunately, in the process of searching for the ultimate sexual experience, it is easy for us to forget the purpose of sexuality. When this happens, the gift of love is replaced by the goal of self-gratification, and the act of love becomes merely an act.

CHILDREN

The modern family is also required to make choices about offspring—choices that were either impossible or inappropriate prior to the present era. Put simply, among the ancients, most married couples did not make decisions about childbearing. Children just came. Many of them. In most cases, children were considered a very valuable component of the family, adding to the security and productive power of the family unit. Thus when the psalmist said that "children are a gift from God" (Psalm 127:3 LB), he was not articulating a religious platitude but a functional reality; children were considered an economic and social blessing. To this generalization, of course, there have been exceptions: some cultures have practiced infanticide under certain circumstances and the upper classes (the precursors of modernity—the only ones with "choice") have always had "child control" options unavailable to the masses. But on the whole, children were a welcome commodity. Indeed, their absence was considered a monumental calamity.

All this sounds quite foreign to modern ears, of course, and for good reason. The status of children has changed quite dramatically in the modern world. For one thing, children no longer have economic value. Indeed, rather than contributing to the family coffers, modern children drain them considerably. Moreover, because they often desert the premises on their eighteenth birthday (when they *finally* become relatively competent and productive), children provide little in the way of old-age security for their progenitors. Old-age heartache is a more likely possibility. And loneliness.

Small wonder, then, that the first question confronting the modern couple is, "Should we have children?" Little wonder, as well, that often the answer is no. If one should ask such couples why they deny themselves the joys of parenthood, one will discover numerous rationales. Some will point to demographics, noting that "the world is already overpopulated." Others, decrying the state of world affairs, may say that they "don't want to bring any more children into a world of violence, poverty, and nuclear proliferation." Some might even be honest and explain that children are too expensive or an encumbrance on parental careers. Whatever the explanation, the fact remains that childlessness is a modern option—a possibility for the modern couple. But to the ancients, it was a curse from God.

Assuming one wants children, a variety of questions still remain: "How many children do we want?" (*"One* would be easy, but he or she will need a playmate; two would be perfect, but *everyone* is having two these days; three would be novel but really a bit much.") "How closely should the children be spaced?" ("Dr. Zajonc says our children will have higher I.Q.s if they're spaced further apart, but, goodness, I'd like to get the last one out of the house before I'm sixty!") "Which gender do we prefer?" ("Look, Mary, if we calculate this thing just right, the probability of our being able to choose the sex of the child goes way up! Now let's see, if you're going to be fertile in about forty-eight hours, then we'd better .... Mary? Mary?! Where *did* she go?")

Finally, there is the possibility of changing one's mind about choices already made. Children can be aborted. This, of course, is in no sense a purely modern possibility. Babies have been "terminated" throughout the ages, often immediately upon delivery. What is different about the modern abortion, however, is that it can be more discreetly performed and more readily obtained. No one needs to know about the pregnancy, and there are few telltale physical effects for the mother. Abortions can be accomplished quickly and imperceptibly—totally outside the context of community. This does at least two things. First, it makes the modern abortion a much more viable alternative— a genuine option for far more people. Second, it transforms the abortion decision from a community/family matter into a solely personal issue. The first point, of course, simply means that abortion is one more choice confronted by the modern family. The second? That is a choice substantially unconstrained by the moral authority of the larger community.

LONGEVITY

How long shall we remain married? That may be the most modern question of all. For we live in an era in which there are a multitude of questions not only about the nature of family relationships, but also about their longevity. Should we stay married? If so, for how long and for what reason? These are the choices of the modern couple.

Divorce, however, is not new. It pervades human history and crosses the bounds of nearly all cultures. Often it has been the prerogative of the rich and the powerful—both to use it and to skirt its implications. In patriarchal societies, for example, men of wealth sometimes used their status to manipulate law and custom, sloughing off an unwanted wife. In most cases, however—and for most of the population—regardless of its form, marriage involved a permanent set of obligations, not only for the marriage partners but also for members of the extended family or larger community. This was especially true in rural areas where, until the modern era, most of earth's humanity lived. Divorce did occur, but it was a serious matter evoking a negative communal response.

For Peter Peasant, then, "till death do us part" was more than a trite phrase in an archaic sacrament. It had functional and symbolic significance. He may not have appreciated its ramifications; indeed, he may have wished with all his might that the miserable promise did not exist. But he lived with the knowledge that he was bound by tradition and duty to his spouse.

By contrast, we moderns live with no such knowledge. In fact, we live with a whole different data set. What we know is that marriages fail. Often. Evidence of such failure, moreover, is not limited to "others"— in other areas or other towns or other families. The evidence of failure pervades our daily existence. Children grow up with such knowledge, date with such knowledge, and get married with such knowledge. In some neighborhoods—and churches—the child who has not had some personal encounter with the consequences of divorce is an anomaly. In most neighborhoods, the possibility of escaping the evidence of marital failure is nonexistent.

For our purposes, the important point is not simply that divorce happens, but that it happens regularly and often. As a result, for the modern man or woman, divorce is not just a theoretical idea. It is an existential fact. At all times, in every modern marriage, the possibility of divorce is a clear and present danger. In the midst of every argument, it is a possible solution. In the midst of every flirtation, it is a conceivable consequence. In the midst of every hardship, it is a tempting way out.

Such a possibility, of course, affects each of us differently, depending on our circumstances. If I am the spouse at my wits' end with an argumentative partner, or tempted by the delights of another mate, or bearing the burden of a dispirited or crippled consort, then the option of divorce means for me the possibility of escape—the chance to leave my troubles behind. On the other hand, if I am the spouse whose opinions are not appreciated, or whose charms are not enough, or whose attributes are less than the societal ideal, then the option of divorce means that I might—at any moment—find myself alone. Quite alone. And that is a frightening possibility in the modern world.

six / The Family of Fear

From what we have seen, it is clear that the modern family, like modern religion, is confronted with a myriad of decisions about all kinds of matters, from the infinitesimal ("Who's going to clean up the doggy-do?") to the grand ("Will you marry me?") and grave ("Won't you please get out of my life?"). Moreover, in making these decisions, family members are—in contrast to their ancestors—far less encumbered by tradition. Rather, they are guided primarily by social forces they do not understand (fads, fashions, class, status, power, etc.) and individual self-interests to which they will not admit.

Social Sources of Familial Choicism

Before proceeding to look at some of the consequences of "choicism" for the modern family, we need to understand its reason for being. Why is the modern family so thoroughly permeated with choices?

As we noted earlier, one of the most salient features of modernity is "mobility." Modern societies are filled with people on the move, not only for the sake of temporary amusement (vacations, for example) but also in an effort to change the location of their homes. There are numerous reasons for this mobile mania, but two seem particularly important.

First, the industrialization process that accompanied (and substantially inspired) modernization has provided us with the technological means for mobility. Until the modern era, humans wishing to travel long distances had to endure immense hardships (unless, of course, they were wealthy). Travel by foot, animal, buggy, or boat was slow, risky, and physically exhausting. It was an ordeal most wished to avoid. By contrast, today it is possible to move half-way around the world without so much as raising a bead of sweat; thus it is relatively easy and inexpensive to change one's place of residence in the modern world.

Second, the economic changes that led to industrialization gave us not only the technological means for mobility but also the reasons for it. We *want* a better job. We *need* to expand our business. We *must* have a larger home. The list of reasons is endless. These reasons for mobility, moreover, are especially enticing in modern societies because of one other technological marvel—modern communication systems. Not only may we want a better job, but we can go on a world-wide hunt to secure one. We can scour the newspapers for them, telephone around the world to inquire concerning them, and fly out for an interview at a moment's notice. Such communication and travel possibilities, then, make it extremely easy for us to relocate. They provide us with unlimited opportunities for job advancement or alternative lifestyles—opportunities that modern men and women, with modern-size appetites for "other possibilities," seem unable to resist.

As we noted earlier, high rates of mobility are significant because whenever human beings change their place of residence, they are confronted with a legion of decisions. These include not only decisions about where to live but also how to live and with whom. Questions emerge about where to worship, shop, go on vacation, have fun, and go to school; with whom to socialize, live, and share; how to dress, behave, and pronounce (or drop) one's r's. In short, the modern mover is bombarded with a host of choices that the permanent resident rarely has to make. A better way of putting it, perhaps, is that—on a great variety of matters—the modern mover makes decisions while the permanent resident relies on tradition.

The long-term effect of mobility is a different way of life. Traditions, which were helpful to the ancients, become irrelevant (or burdensome) to the inhabitants of modernity. Instead of relying on traditions to guide us through the day, we moderns make individual decisions, theoretically calculated to bring us the greatest possible pleasure and fulfillment. As a result, community gives way to individual pursuit, the taken-for-granted world is replaced by a calculating world view, and traditions are eclipsed by a multitudinous number of choices.

One last point. The most fundamental reason we moderns are plagued with an overabundance of choices is that we are a choice-seeking people. We want more alternatives, more options, more possibilities. That is why we seek technologies that increase our options. That is why we move whenever it suits our bank accounts. That is why we change spouses, houses, and neighbors whenever we think it will make us happier. In traditional societies, the human appetite for more choices was curbed by the social setting. In a sense, traditional social structures said, "No! You must live within a limited set of possibilities—within a certain tradition." In contrast, the modern social setting says, "Yes!" Yes to dreams of other living conditions. Yes to hopes of better relationships. Yes to a life of more and more alternatives and fewer and fewer restrictions. Instead of constraining our desire for choices, modernity manages only to encourage it. Such social seduction we humans find difficult to resist.

INSECURITY

For the modern family, the implications of choicism go far beyond the simple existence of numerous decision-making opportunities. If the only consequence of familial choicism was the need to make more decisions, we might consider it a burden but hardly a significant problem. In fact, however, the modern preoccupation with familial alternatives has not only burdened us with an overwhelming number of decisions, but it has also played havoc with the human condition.

The single most problematic element of the modern family is its instability. Individuals are not predictable. We feel different on Monday than we do on Tuesday; we want something desperately on Saturday night that we hardly care about the next morning. Our emotions ebb and flow—with the moon, our blood-sugar level, and our acne condition. The car that made my heart race five years ago, today seems like a bloated heifer. The skinny girl I scorned in eighth grade is presently earning millions as a model. People change. The things that affect people change. The standards on which people make judgments change. When the stability of the family is dependent on the transient feelings of individuals, its doom is sure.

This, of course, is not a new revelation. Most of us are aware of the whimsical nature of our own choices. And therein lies the rub. To know that one's family is (and will be) the consequence of one's own decisions—and not the outgrowth of tradition—is to know insecurity. Personal histories are not kind. They reveal scads of decisions that, upon reflection, we brand as rash, stupid, or worse. From them, we receive little assurance that future decisions will be altogether imbued with wisdom—little assurance, that is, that a family created out of our own choices will be satisfactory to us tomorrow.

Far more frightening than our own decisions, however, are the decisions of "significant others." It is one thing to worry about my own fallibility; it is quite another to worry about human frailty in others. The problem, of course, is control. When I make choices, I know they can be bad ones, but at least I can exercise some degree of control over them. Granted, this control is more than a bit illusory, given the impact of emotions and circumstances on my decisions. Nevertheless, at least a modicum of personal control is present, and, if one works at it hard enough, maybe even more than that.

The choices of others, however, are ultimately out of our control. Regardless of our own charisma or influence (and setting aside the possibility of coercion for the moment), we cannot guarantee the decisions of others. This is why we are frightened by presidents or party secretaries who exercise control over nuclear catastrophe. This is why we are frightened by spouses, parents, and children who exercise control over family catastrophe.

Spouse

To know that one is free to marry the spouse of one's own choosing is also to know that one is free to dissolve the union (that is, if one takes solemn marriage vows lightly). Regardless of the moral pressures a couple may feel to stay married, if they alone were responsible for initiating the marriage, then they alone will be responsible for its longevity. As a result, the freedom we so cherish during dating and courtship is a haunting specter throughout the marriage relationship. It means that at any moment one may lose one's spouse—whether because of impulse or because of reason.

Such a possibility is quite different from death, the other specter that looms over every relationship. Death is both inevitable and socially acceptable. One is not blamed for losing a spouse by death, and there are social conventions (even in the modern era) designed to help the grieving party.

Divorce, however prevalent, is not socially acceptable and there is little social support for those who endure it. Because it stems from a host of personal decisions, moreover (including the decision to marry the turkey in the first place), it carries with it the burden of failure. Those who live through a modern divorce cannot escape feeling culpable, regardless of whether or not they publicly acknowledge such feelings. The logic of choicism demands it. To be free to choose is to be responsible for choices made. That is why the world of choice is a world teeming not only with insecurity but also with guilt.

Children

If insecurity is a problem for the modern spouse, it is doubly so for the modern child. While the spouse must worry about the decisions of a mate, the child must contemplate the possible consequences of two choice-makers: Either parent may destroy the marriage and launch the family into uncharted waters. Since children are in a wholly dependent relationship with their parents, marital stability is a matter in which they have little influence but a great deal of investment. Obviously, the modern child is in a highly precarious position.

The feeling of insecurity, however, is something of a learned trait. Its presence depends on an awareness of catastrophic possibilities. From day one, the child learns to "worry" about a wide range of possibilities— from the consequences of food deprivation (hunger) to falling from heights (pain). Both nature and parents use such "worries" to promote certain types of behavior (sleep) and discourage others (crawling out of cribs). This can be an effective teaching device as long as the child has some degree of control over the potentially worrisome happening; a child can deal with the worry of falling out of the crib, for example, if she can link the worry with behavior (e.g., pulling oneself over the side of the crib) and control the behavior.

A feeling of insecurity results when there is no perceived link between the worry and behavior. The best example here may be the threat of nuclear war. Most children and adults probably perceive little relationship between their own actions and the possibility of a nuclear holocaust. Yet they know that a nuclear nightmare is a genuine possibility, one that would most likely bring about their death. Therefore, because they have no control over a matter of paramount importance to them, a feeling of insecurity is a reasonable response.

A sense of insecurity is also a reasonable response to the possibility of divorce. Divorce is something over which children assume little or no control, yet it can unalterably change their lives. Like nuclear war, it would have devastating consequences. Like nuclear war, its occurrence would result from the personal decisions of others. Unlike nuclear war, however, it is a common occurrence in the modern era and therefore a much more viable possibility to the child of the modern family.

The last point is important. It not only means that insecurity is a much more likely possibility for the child of the modern marriage, but also that—for the parent—buffering a child from such insecurity is a nearly futile endeavor. When a modern child wakes up in the middle of the night, in tears because of a nuclear nightmare, the parent can hold the child and say—with at least a modicum of historical integrity— "Everything's going to be all right." To say those same words to the modern child undergoing a nightmare of divorce is an almost meaningless activity, regardless of the good intentions or solid commitments of the parent. The words are mocked by the realities of everyday life.

I clearly remember when I first became aware of this modern reality. It was the day I had to tell my children about the separation and impending divorce of two of our closest friends. Suddenly for our children divorce was not a theoretical possibility anymore—something that happened only to "other" people. It was a live option, even in our circle of friends. At the time, I remember my own feelings of anger and resentment—not at our friends, certainly, whose own pain and suffering I felt deeply—but at a situation that had forced me to plunge a modern fact into the hearts of our children. I resented it because I knew their world would never again seem so stable. I resented it because never again would they feel quite so secure. I resented it because, regardless of the number or quality of our assurances to the contrary, they now had to live with the possibility of their own parents' divorce. If it could happen to close friends (whose love for them was genuine beyond doubt), it could happen to their parents. That is the pernicious and inescapable conclusion of the modern child.

Others

We tend to think family instability is a problem only for members of the nuclear family—for parents and those children still living at home. Such thinking reveals our modernity as well as our ignorance. It stems both from a very limited notion of what a family is and from an inability to see fully the rippling effect of broken relationships.

In the modern era a family is commonly thought of as those individuals who live together under one roof—usually, one or two parents and their under-age offspring. Such a conception seems limited if we remember that, for Peter Peasant, the family always included grandparents and usually extended to in-laws, cousins, and a variety of adopted persons (e.g., children of deceased parents). Whatever the exact nature of the family—and of course it varied widely—the family included much more than parents and helpless children.

But one does not have to reach into traditional societies in order to perceive the limited notion of the modern family: it ought to be apparent to any living adult. For example, a forty-year-old with a spouse and two adolescent children ought to be aware that his or her "family" is not confined to those individuals residing in the "home." Such an individual probably has living parents (living perhaps only God knows where), brothers and sisters (ditto), all of whom are a part of the family. Of course, we may try to ignore this fact by calling these folk our "other" or "previous" family, as if they were two distinct groups of people, or as if we were somehow aborted from the former arrangement. This modern ability to play word games, however, is quite uninteresting. The interesting thing is our willingness to believe in them.

Believing that the modern nuclear family fully contains "the family" is, of course, a convenient notion. It enables us to ignore some of the broader effects of family instability and thereby relieves us of a certain amount of guilt. If I can convince myself, for example, that, besides being my concern, a divorce is also the legitimate concern of only my spouse and our children, then I can limit my "worries" to those individuals. In practical terms, this means that if I am considering the possibility of divorcing my spouse, I need not bother myself with its effects on other people. "Others" are not legitimately involved.

But, in fact, others are involved. Since the seventeenth century, no one has more eloquently expressed that truth than John Donne, quite possibly because he was the last to really believe it: "No man is an Iland, intire of it selfe; every man is a peece of the Continent, a part of the maine; if a Clod bee washed away by the Sea, Europe is the lesse, as well as if a Promontorie were, as well as if a Mannor of thy friends or of thine owne were." When a marriage fractures, it tears apart far more than a nuclear family.

It rips at hearts. Few people know the pain, for example, of a parent watching the dissolution of a son's or daughter's marriage. It is a grief that sometimes parallels the loss of a spouse. And yet the modern person must ask why? Why does this cause pain in someone so uninvolved—one outside of the nuclear family? The answer, of course, is love. Who in God's creation loves like a parent? Whose love is more altruistic? More sacrificial? More unsolicitous of reward? More concerned about effect? It is because the love of a parent knows no measure that a parent's grief is equally keen. Such an explanation, of course, mocks the modern notion of "family," since it admits to a lifelong relationship between parent and child. Thus apologists for modernity like to interpret such parental grief as an expression of self-interest (parents attempting to live their lives vicariously through their children). In doing so, however, they miss a larger truth— one easily overlooked in the modern world: broken relationships break the heart.

CONCLUSION

When I had to tell my children about the divorce of our close friends, their reaction was only momentarily emotional. The long-term effect was a new way of thinking about family relationships. Such relationships were no longer a fact of life to be taken for granted. They were, instead, frail things, susceptible not only to the ravages of death but also to the human touch. For child and adult alike, the fractured family means that even the most dependable relationships are not dependable in the modern world. Like the job from which one may be fired and the love for which one may be spurned, the modern family is a thing that simply may be lost. In a world of precarious relationships, only a fool would consider the family a safe haven. Indeed, it is itself nothing more than another set of precarious relationships—the perfect breeding ground for rampant insecurity.

seven / The Family of Fantasy

Insecurity is an odd sort of thing, its consequences manifestly unpredictable. Burdened under its weight, some are driven to their knees, forced to acknowledge their own inadequacies before a sovereign God. For others, the burden of insecurity is too great, its weight more than the human spirit can bear. For the latter, insecurity's yoke is less the affliction that leads to glory than a hard taskmaster, driving them, not to their knees, but to the edge of sanity.

Somewhere between these two poles lies the majority of humanity—unable to acknowledge their Creator but unwilling to follow the logic of their insanity. For these, modernity offers two escapes from familial insecurity. The first I call the illusion of the *self-fulfilling family.*

ILLUSION I: THE SELF-FULFILLING FAMILY

One reaction to insecurity is huddling. Sometimes, when we feel threatened by external events or anxious about our own situation, we respond by drawing together with those around us. Like the football squad that huddles to plan strategy, we know that our chances of success greatly improve if we work as a team. There is safety in numbers. We huddle for our own protection and defense.

The huddling response can, of course, lead to a genuinely enjoyable experience, especially when it is initiated by something other than deep insecurity. Most of us, for example, have had the pleasure of drawing together for a short time in order to achieve a specific goal. Whether it is for the purpose of winning an athletic contest, raising funds for a worthy cause, or defending a cherished value, such an experience can be extremely fulfilling. Indeed, after it is over, one sometimes concludes that the "huddling experience" was more important than the project that initiated the experience in the first place. In a world of relational scarcity, huddling can be a welcome relief from the daily routine.

A relief, but not an answer. Huddling is designed to be a short-term answer to a particular problem—a brief interlude in the conundrum of life in order to deal with a specific threat or need. When it lives beyond its usefulness, however, huddling is no longer a relief or an answer. It is a genuinely dangerous thing, distracting us from responsibilities and disfiguring the human image.

Unfortunately, for the inhabitants of the modern family, huddling is an especially attractive response. The

modern world *is*, after all, a perilous environment for
the family. Its choices, illusive freedoms, vacuous traditions, and seductive possibilities all tug away at the
fabric of family relationships. Little wonder, then, that
the ꞏꞏꞏderns most concerned about the state of the
contemporary family often adopt a lifestyle very much
akin to huddling. They are simply trying to protect
themselves from the pillage of modernity. Sometimes
they have even been known to call themselves Christians.

Familial huddling assumes, first, that nothing is as
important as the nuclear family and, second, that all
one's needs can be met within the context of the nuclear family. The latter point suggests that the modern
family is supposed to be one's only source of affection, shelter, love, sustenance, physical care, etc. The
first point means that every activity is perceived in
terms of its relationship to the family. One's occupation, for example, is evaluated in terms of its contribu-
tion to the family welfare; political decisions are based
on family interests; religious involvement is aimed exclusively at strengthening the nuclear family; and residential patterns are determined by the assumed needs
of the family. By making the family the hub around
which all other activities revolve, it is hoped that family relationships will be strengthened and the family
unit will become impervious to the onslaughts of modernity.

Although this response to modernity is reasonable, it
is also highly problematic. For one thing, I doubt that
it is a realizable ideal. Most families do not have the
resources, time, creativity, or stamina to live up to the
expectations of the self-fulfilling family. More importantly, however, it is wrong. Like anything else in
God's creation, the family is not to be worshiped.
When we make the nuclear family the center of our
existence, we overburden it with responsibilities,

underutilize other institutions, and run the risk of living closed, selfish lives.

Why is this so? First, the nuclear family cannot meet all our needs nor is it supposed to. The husband needs relationships with other men; wives need relationships with other women; children need relationships with other children. Moreover, all of them need relationships with the elderly, singles, neighbors, work partners, the poor, and extended-family members—not to mention members of the local church. The nuclear family is (by historical standards) an extremely narrowly defined entity. As a result, it is well suited to meet the relational needs of parents and children, but ill equipped to handle the variety of other relationships for which we are also responsible. Those of us who find our *only* fulfillment in the nuclear family, therefore, will be something less than whole people—and far from the intentions, I believe, of the One who designed us.

Second, when the nuclear family is worshiped, such worship inevitably undermines the purposes of other legitimate social institutions. If the family is of ultimate importance, then all other institutions (such as government, church, and neighborhood) are, by comparison, trivial. This leads not only to the neglect of a variety of important human issues (such as the need for justice, the proclamation of God's Word, and love of neighbor), but it also skews one's understanding of these other institutions. Many advocates of the nuclear family, for example, view politics purely in terms of its relationship to the perceived interests of the family. As a result, they cast their ballots for political candidates whom they consider to be profamily, failing to take into account the candidate's broader world view. It does no good, however, to vote for a politician who is profamily if he or she is at the same time opposed to public justice or the value of human life. Indeed, it does a great deal of harm.

Finally, the huddling nuclear family is, at bottom, a very selfish cadre of human beings. Its members view the world from their own perspectives, wholly in terms of the family's concerns. From such a vantage point, husbands (and wives) have justified shady business deals, wives (and husbands) have ignored the needs of the poor, children have attended racist schools, and families have lived in splendid isolation from the cries of the oppressed. All this, and more, has been done in the name of the "family." Surely it is one of the great ironies of our time that some of those who seek to protect the family from the ravages of modernity do so at the expense of their own brothers and sisters. Nothing could be more disastrous to the cause of genuine community nor more ameliorating to the ulterior motives of modernity.

Illusion II: The Other-directed Fantasy

There is a modern alternative to the self-fulfilling family, however, and it is every bit as seductive as the first familial illusion. Its focus is not on the possibilities of fulfillment within one's own family, but on the fulfilling possibilities of other relationships. It is the illusion of the *other-directed fantasy.*

Huddling is only one response to insecurity; another is projection. While some of us cling to family members in our moment of need, others of us accuse those same individuals of causing our problems. This tendency to accuse is one of the more unreasonable human inclinations, in my opinion. Precisely at the moment when we are most in need of comfort from others, we lash out and blame them for our own inadequacies.

Most of us, I think, have experienced projection, either as its target or perhaps its carrier. I know, for example, that I am most likely to be irritable toward my wife and children when I am anxious about my

115

own condition or situation. Indeed, it is for that reason that, when I am sick, I am a terrible patient. Family members attempt to console me and the best I can do is tell them to go away; more likely, I accuse them of improper service ("The tea is cold!") or insufficient sympathy ("You have no idea how awful I feel!"). At times, I even manage to blame them for my own affliction ("You gave me this flu bug, you know!"). Forty-eight hours later, after the flu is gone, I am the milk of loving kindness (*my* idea of loving kindness, anyway).

I am not a psychologist and have thus been spared the knowledge of why human beings do such ludicrous things (reason enough, I believe, to become a sociologist)—I do not know all the hoary little explanations for humanity's projective propensities nor why some of us are especially prone to use projection. This I do know, however: it is precisely in those moments when insecurity turns to projection that we are most vulnerable to the illusion of the other-directed fantasy.

This vulnerability is predicated on two factors. First, to project one's inadequacies on others is to make those same "others" responsible for one's own difficulties and problems. Spouses, children, and parents—not to mention pastors, teachers, and friends—become something of a personal repository of ill will. They are the reason for one's problems, the causes of one's frustration, the source of one's defeats. In short, if we are insecure about our own living arrangement, projection allows us to blame it on those with whom we are living.

Second, the modern carrier of projection inhabits a society of vast alternatives. This means that at exactly the moment my heart is blaming my difficulties on parent, spouse, or child, society is whispering in my ear, "Things could be different: you could have a more charming husband, one who would never insult you or complain about your spending habits." Or, "You could have a less liberated wife, the kind who would live for you and appreciate your many accomplishments." Or, "You could have more amiable children if you had a spouse who took parental responsibilities more seriously, or, better yet, your life could be child-free, without any parental responsibilities at all." Or, "You could have a life free from parental harassment, unencumbered by the hassle of dumb rules and dumber parents." Yes, indeed, life could be very different.

The point is, we moderns live in a world where an alternative family is not only imaginable; it is a seductive, well-articulated possibility. The distinction is an important one. Human beings of all ages have been able to dream of living other lives, in different worlds and relationships. Chroniclers and bards aplenty have made their living off this particular human capacity. Modernity's peculiarity is that it mass produces alternative images and pronounces them good. These images are plastered across billboards and the pages of newspapers, animated on television and theater screens, and driven home in lively stereo on radios, records, and cassettes—all totally desirable, attractive, and possible.

Most importantly, possible. Possible, because old arrangements can be easily aborted. Possible, because few traditions are strong enough to exert a constraining influence. Possible, because alternatives are at the heart of the modern vision.

There is, of course, one other possibility in the other-directed fantasy—one less talked about, certainly, but every bit as probable. It is the possibility of failure. Indeed, when we cut ourselves off from old relationships in search of new and, theoretically, more fulfilling ones, we set ourselves up for failure. Why? Because, for one thing, reality cannot possibly match the dreams of the other-directed fantasy. This is true not only because modernity bombards us with unrealistic possibilities but also because we human beings do not dream realities; we dream dreams. That is precisely why we need traditions—not to squelch dreams, but to constrain them, to keep them from undermining the creature who brought them into fruition in the first place.

Our quest of the other-directed fantasy is doomed for another reason also: it takes place in the midst of modernity. One must remember that modernity is not on the side of relationships that are "true, good, and beautiful"; these are only the forms it uses to present relational choices. Rather, modernity is doggedly on the side of alternatives and better possibilities. At every point in time, modernity works against choices made in the past (commitments) and at the behest of future alternatives (possibilities). The moment Martin Modern seizes the fruit of a new relational opportunity, therefore, the new relationship is transformed from a future possibility into a historical reality and becomes the enemy of modernity. Now the former fantasy becomes a commitment. Now the new relationship must be judged in the light of other possibilities. Now the other-directed fantasy must be experienced in the context of *other* other-directed fantasies. What modernity lacks in honesty, it makes up for in logic. It is, unfortunately, the logic of an illusion.

No Weak People

In the end, however, the greatest tragedy of the modern family may not be that it presents us with choices too numerous to comprehend or that it leaves its members insecure and in quest of illusions. The greatest tragedy may be that the modern family has no place for the weak.

Not everyone is displeased with modernity, of

course. For those who are convinced that "you only go around once in life"—that "life is for the living" and "you've got to grab the gusto" while you can; for those who think that "you've got to look out for Ol' Number One" and that the singular purpose of humanity is self-fulfillment (whether in the guise of realization or actualization); for those willing to place personal interests above relational commitments and the needs of others; for those who are young, beautiful, and strong—for all of these the world of modernity may be a bit of a gas. Indeed, they may consider it their oyster.

For the oyster, however, the modern world portends a very different kind of existence. It is a place where homes are routinely dislodged, where protective traditions are splayed with enthusiasm and discarded with contempt (though sometimes retained as quaint decorations), where relational pearls are plundered for profit, and where one's very being is the consuming desire of another's insatiable appetite. In such a world, it is not fun to be an oyster. And yet, the world of the modern family is teeming with oysters.

Oysters of the other-directed fantasy

Living with those in quest of the other-directed fantasy is a precarious existence, to say the least. For the dependent spouse, it means constantly living with the possibility of rejection and isolation. For dependent children, it means living with the possibility of social chaos—the loss of their world. For one who is emotionally, financially, or physically dependent on other family members, the illusion of the other-directed fantasy is a threat to their very existence. The modern family is no place for the needy.

Nor is it a great place for those who fail to meet the standards of the modern familial illusion—that of being fit, firm, fun, and fulfilling. My own biased assessment of the population between the ages of eighteen and thirty-five would suggest that perhaps a third of them meet such standards (but only marginally), and another third might be able to convince themselves that—with the help of cosmetologists, beauticians, masseuses, psychiatrists, plastic surgeons, and others ad infinitum—they could possibly deceive another into believing they meet such standards (most likely someone who is attempting the same deception in reverse). For the final third, however, there is clearly no hope. If this is true—and it seems to me a rather conservative estimate—then *at least* a third of those in the prime of their life ought to feel excluded from the dream of the modern family.

Given the pathological nature of that dream, we might be tempted to congratulate such folk. After all, fulfilling the dream is not exactly a guarantee of happiness. We need to remember, however, that the standards of the dream are those both in which they have been instructed and by which they will be judged. The point is, not that they have opted out of the dream, but they have been banished from it. Chances are, they long for the dream. Realities are, it has no place for them.

Oysters of the self-fulfilling family

If the illusion of the other-directed fantasy tends to exclude those lacking in personal qualities (e.g., independence, beauty, wit), then one might say that the illusion of the self-fulfilling family excludes those who are weak by position. Since the self-fulfilling family of the modern era is a nuclear family, consisting only of parents and minor children, all those who find themselves outside these two roles also find themselves excluded from the family. This includes the aged, the widowed, the divorced, those who never married, those adults incapacitated by special needs, and anyone else considered a threat or irrelevant to the concerns of the self-fulfilling family (the poor, the imprisoned, the oppressed, etc.).

Both the scope and the pain of this modern tendency was brought home to me when I was still in college. Enrolled in an Urban Studies Seminar, I was required to visit numerous institutions in a metropolitan area. One of these was a home for the elderly located in an old hotel in the heart of a deteriorating section of the city. As I strolled around inside the building and talked with the tenants, I became increasingly struck by their isolation from the modern family. Of those with whom I chatted, none had seen their children in over a year, most far longer than that. A majority had no idea where their children were living nor how to contact them in an emergency. They frankly informed me that their children considered them a nuisance; some had been explicitly told to stay out of their child's life (as if they had a choice). And so there they sat, in splendid isolation, waiting to die—without purpose, function, or the company of those whom they had nurtured.

Not all retirement homes are like this, of course, nor are all their inhabitants so thoroughly cut off from their children. Nevertheless, such institutions are quintessentially modern. They bear testimony to the need of the modern family to "do something" with individuals who—by dint of age, status, or position—fail to fit the parameters of the self-fulfilling family. The fact that some institutions and/or offspring handle the matter more kindly than others, then, is somewhat irrelevant to the point (though certainly not to the elderly themselves): the modern family ideal simply does not include old people, and thus emerges the need to find another place for them.

The aged, however, are only one example. A nuclear family that is in hot pursuit of its own fulfillment also ignores single adults. Some singles, of course, wish to be excluded, and in the modern context, their wish is granted with a vengeance. Many, however, are not single by desire but by circumstance (death of a spouse, divorce, unrequited love, etc.). For these, the exclusionary inclinations of the modern family sometimes means living a life of loneliness and social ostracism. Such is often the case even for those who are single by choice—especially those who wish not to live in a singles encampment and who desire relationships with children, peer parents, and older adults. But where can they go for such relationships? Their parents? *They* are probably locked up in Sun City. Their married friends? These friends are no doubt absorbed in the self-fulfilling family. The local church? It is probably composed of one hundred self-fulfilling nuclear families, with many of its sermons, services, and functions being aimed entirely at the needs of the modern family.

Victims of the self-fulfilling family also include the poor and the dispossessed, not because they are necessarily without family (though many are), but because they are outside the interests and concerns of the modern family. The huddling family, remember, is bent on self-preservation. It attempts to deflect the arrows of modernity through self-absorption. As a result, it tends to isolate itself in neighborhoods with other huddling families, thereby removing its members from daily interaction with the disadvantaged. The huddling family does not touch the poor nor hear cries of the oppressed nor smell the stench of a tenement building. Its only exposure to the disadvantaged is through the media—which present them as one more modern "problem" from which the self-fulfilling family needs to be protected. It means, as well, that the modern family has claimed another victim, not because its inhabitants lack compassion, necessarily, but because its design will not allow them to express it.

Conclusion

What kind of a family is it that offers satisfaction only to the strong—whose vision excludes the weak and makes self-gratification a virtue?

What kind of family is it that drives its members by the dual illusions of the self-fulfilling family and the other-directed fantasy—all the while mocking the constraints and curbs of tradition?

What kind of family is it that renders its inhabitants frightened by the choices of others and worried about their own—whose relationships are so tentative that they provide nothing in the way of security, much less genuine fulfillment?

To be sure, it is something less than a community. It is the modern family.

PART IV / **Community in Christian Perspective**

eight / **Relationships**

From what we have seen, community in the modern world is not only a phenomenon under assault, it is also a concept virtually without meaning. Its elements of tradition, vision, and relationships are radically attenuated by the social conditions of modernity, and its modern manifestations in family and religion bear little resemblance to the communities of ages past. Under such conditions, it would seem prudent to ask, first, what ought the Christian to think about the modern demise of community and, second, what can be done about it once it is understood.

The first question is really the most important. Not

only is it incumbent on us to think about community in Christian categories but it is important to do so *before* we decide on a course of action. We have already noted that it is the modern tendency to concentrate on the means rather than the ends—the hows rather than the whats or whys. We must resist that impulse if at all possible.

Moreover, it is essential to engage in such deliberation because what we think about a particular subject (in this case, community) will affect our behavior. I am not a social determinist. Though I believe social forces exert strong influences on our thinking and doing, I am also convinced that our thinking gives shape to the social world around us. Thus the fact that we have nothing like genuine community in the modern world is not merely the result of autonomous social forces beyond our control. It is, rather, the result of a great variety of factors, one of which involves the choices made (or defaulted on) by a great many human beings. If we are to confront the problem of community in any meaningful fashion, therefore, we must carefully reflect on the efficacy of modern social conditions, not as a people trapped by those conditions, but as Christians who trust in a Reality much larger than the one now encumbering us.

Our goal in part IV, therefore, is to think Christianly about the basic elements of community. Of what significance are relationships to the Christian? What is the value and import of tradition, not simply to those who desire community, but for those who truly want their lives influenced by a Christian world view? And what kind of vision, if any, ought to permeate the Christian's understanding of community? These are the questions that beg our attention as we seek to grapple with the social implications of the Christian faith in the midst of modernity.

RELATIONSHIPS

When we look to the biblical record for an understanding of human relationships, there are a variety of passages that beckon our attention. We might, for example, want to focus on the ingredients of human relationships and look to Scripture for counsel on how we ought to relate to one another. Such an investigation will reveal, quite quickly, I suspect, that the single most salient element in any human encounter is love (1 Corinthians 13). Beyond that, there are numerous injunctions stressing the importance of relationships that are just (Isaiah 56:1), holy (Leviticus 11:44), and rooted in a concern for the welfare of others (Matthew 19:19). The qualities that constitute the fruit of the Spirit are listed, in part, as relational guidelines whose purpose is to inform us of how we ought to act toward others. Love, patience, kindness, self-control, goodness, and gentleness, for example, are not only evidences of Christ's Spirit in us, but they are the ingredients of healthy relationships. They are the biblical parameters for social intercourse.

Our concern at this time, however, is not so much with how we ought to relate to one another as with how we should conceive of human relationships themselves: What is the fundamental picture of human relationships presented in Scripture? Of what importance are relationships to the God of the universe? Of what importance ought they be to us?

For the answers to these questions, I believe we must not focus on biblical ethics but on a biblical understanding of who we are as human beings. And for that, we must return to the Book on Beginnings and be prepared to take its account of creation quite seriously.

In the Beginning

Within the first two chapters of Genesis, three significant things are said about human relationships. First, in Genesis 1:1 we read, "In the beginning God created the heavens and the earth." After that, in verse 26 God says, "Let us make man in our image, in our likeness." Finally, in 2:18 the Lord makes this rather amazing statement: "It is not good for the man to be alone. I will make him a helper suitable for him." If we take each of these statements in turn, I think we will catch a glimpse of the created relational nature of humanity.

Genesis 1:1

The initial statement simply reminds us that God is the Creator. It is by his hand that all things have their being and it is out of his creative nature that humanity came onto the scene. God is our Maker and Sustainer. That fact alone implies a relationship between us and God. It reminds us that we are not gods, that we did not create ourselves, and that we are not capable of adding even an inch to our stature. Fundamentally, we are dependent on God for our existence. Dependency means vulnerability. Dependency means that my very being is contingent upon the will of God. Dependency means, more than anything else, that a relationship exists between the God of creation and every human being who walks the face of the earth.

Genesis 1:26

This relationship, moreover, is unique within the domain of God's revealed creation. For here is a creature made in the image of the Creator. God duplicated himself in humanity in such a way that human beings have the capacity not only for rational thought, moral experience, and creative expression, but also to be in communion with God. There is the possibility of making a relational choice with regard to the Creator.

With the ability to choose, however, also came certain responsibilities (e.g., "Fill the earth and subdue it." "Till it and keep it." "Of the tree of the knowledge of good and evil you shall not eat" [Genesis 1:28; 2:15-17 RSV]) as well as the necessity of living with the consequences of the choices they made. Thus this relationship with God was not an amorphous thing but one that was established within a specific context. Human beings were designed to relate to God in a certain way.

The fact that God created human beings in his image also implies that we have relational characteristics. Certainly, the Bible presents God as a relationa' Being. Not only has he populated his domain with a multitude of companions (angels of varying descriptions and ranks), but Christian trinitarians believe that God is, in and of himself, a social Being, at the same time One and Three. All of this suggests that God's character is relational in essence and that those whom he created in his image are relational by design.

Genesis 2:18

It is God's explanation of the creation of Eve that is probably the most insightful, relative to the nature of human relationships, and certainly the most amazing. We must remember that when God said, "It is not good for the man to be alone. I will make a helper suitable for him" (Genesis 2:18), Adam already had at his disposal relationships with God and other earthly creatures. But from the Creator's perspective, these relationships were not adequate for Adam; they were not enough to satisfy the relational need that God himself had put into the heart of humanity.

Eve was created, therefore, to complete God's creation, to eradicate the possibility of loneliness, to finish the creation of humankind. What this means, of course, is that human beings need others of their own species by God's decree, that humans were created to relate to one another in a social context, and that this is what God intended for his creation. Aloneness (as a normal state of being) is not good for us; togetherness, on the other hand, is both good and necessary. Companionship, not isolation, is the intended creational norm.

The creation account, then, makes abundantly clear that God designed the human being to be a relational creature. Our social predisposition is not an accident, nor is it a weakness, nor is it the result of depravity or sin. It is, rather, the consequence of God's goodness and love for his creation. It is, in short, a gift of God.

This gift, unfortunately, is not readily appreciated by the recipient. For relationships, like everything else in God's good creation, were dealt a heavy blow by the Fall and the introduction of sin. The full implications of the Fall are clearly beyond the scope of this study. It is important to note, however, that sin placed a terrible warp in the constitution of human relationships. Not only did it alienate us from our Creator but it also severely estranged us from one another. From Cain and Abel onward, the Bible presents a picture of humanity perverting, usurping, and abrogating relational norms.

COMMUNALISM

Especially relevant to any treatise on community are two forms of rational perversion. The first is more characteristic of the world of Peter Peasant, though not unknown to our own. It assumes that the life of the community is of greater significance than the person and that individuals may be justifiably sacrificed for the sake of the community. It upholds the rights of the community over those of the person and, indeed, often attempts to liquidate outbreaks of personal identity altogether. In effect, the person's identity is fused with that of the group's, and the will of the group becomes the will of the person. Conformity is praised, deviance is nearly impossible, and personhood is squelched. This perversion is sometimes called "communalism."

Peter Peasant was particularly susceptible to the effects of communalism because he lived in a social context conducive to its development. For all of the reasons outlined in chapter 2, Peter inhabited a community that was relatively closed and immobile. His world was his community. As a result, those who occupied places of authority (noblemen, priests, parents, etc.) were in a position to use communal relationships for their own interests and profit. Thus a father could use traditional patriarchal relationships to thwart his daughter's marital wishes, a priest could exercise the prerogatives of his religious role to extract exorbitant tithes and gifts, and a lord might use his royal authority to levy burdensome taxes, maintain cheap labor, or confiscate land. Peter Peasant may not have liked his lot. He and his friends may have prayed daily that God would send fire and brimstone upon father, priest, or lord. But if the ethics of communalism were intact, he would have had to accept the situation as a given. In fact, if communalism was operating effectively, he would never even realize that he was being exploited (a condition Marx tagged false consciousness).

For the Christian in a modern pluralistic society, such forms of communalism seem cruel beyond belief. And, of course, they are. One should be quick to note, however, that the problem with communalism does not stem from an overemphasis on relationships but on a misperception of their purpose and a misuse of their potential. By this I mean that Peter Peasant's difficulties at this point are not because community relationships are too deep or too rich or too meaningful. His problem results, instead, from those who are willing to exploit such relationships to serve their own interests (e.g., greedy lords) and from Peter's "willingness" to allow traditional relationships to serve as a justification for such exploitation.

For example, let us say that Peter's father refuses to feed Peter properly because he is a glutton and wants to consume most of the family's food supply himself. Let us further assume that Peter (his stomach to the contrary notwithstanding) accepts this arrangement because he considers his father to be the final authority within the family. Now, clearly such a situation comes into being, not because the relationship between father and son is a good one, but, quite the contrary, because the father is greedy and because the values of communalism legitimate his greed. In other words, when those in authority deny the interests of others, communalism actually undermines rather than supports human relationships.

A genuine relationship seeks mutual benefit, not the satisfaction of only one party (by dint of position). Communalism, however, completely ignores the need for relationships that are just and mutually beneficial, because it values conformity above all else. Though it may masquerade as a solution to the quest for relationships, in reality it is nothing of the sort.

From a biblical perspective, then, we might say that communalism takes the human need for relationships and twists it into an excuse for unjust associations. It uses the God-given desire for belonging and bends it into a demand for conformity. In so doing, it disfigures God's image in people and substantially erodes the purpose of human relationships. Instead of fulfilling people's need for one another, communalism thwarts it and plays the part of the impostor. Although it may quench an immediate thirst for fellowship (as those who run to communalistic cults may discover), in the long run it cannot but leave a craving for genuine relationships.

INDIVIDUALISM

Although communalism is far from absent today (it exists not only in cultic form, but also in the political ideologies of the far left and the far right), it is not the central relational problem of the modern Western world. That status is reserved for another kind of perversion—one that is sometimes termed individualism.

If the chief sin of communalism is its exploitation of human relationships, that of individualism lies in its denial of their importance and necessity. Rather than perverting relationships themselves, individualism perverts the human need for such relationships. Its fundamental assumption is that the individual is of paramount importance and value. Relationships exist for the sake of the individual only; they have no inherent value of their own. Value is singularly ascribed to the self. Its interests, needs, and concerns are the basis on which all decisions are to be made.

Modernity, it turns out, is an ideal breeding ground for individualism. Among the many reasons for this correlation, one seems particularly salient; it concerns the role of choice in modern societies. By emphasizing the importance of choice (in everything from ice cream to marriage partners), modernity creates a climate in which the individual's wishes become the primary focus of attention.

For example, two overriding concerns in modernity are (1) the development of products (a face, figure, personality) that others will want to choose, and (2) the choosing for oneself of commodities that are personally satisfying. Both of these activities focus primarily on the needs of the self. The first requires that I rearrange myself to suit the wishes of others (an other-directed activity designed for the purpose of self-satisfaction), and the second requires that I define my interests as paramount in the selection of appropriate patterns of behavior. In either case, the individual's needs become the central concern in the development of relationships. While self-concern as a basis for relationships is not a modern invention (it's as old as sin), the assumed propriety of such a motivation certainly may be. We are one of the few cultures to make a virtue of egocentrism.

Modern Christians, of course, are not ignorant of this problem. I suspect that selfishness is one of those maladies routinely castigated by nearly every pastor each week of the year. We understand that putting self first is not an especially Christian approach to human relationships. Where we miss the boat, however, is in dealing with it as a purely personal problem—as if the only issue at stake was the extent of an individual's lascivious proclivities. The modern problem, however, is not merely the result of personal inclination. It is also born out of a social context that allows, encourages, and sustains individualistic life-styles.

From a Christian perspective, the taproot of this problem is the modern propensity to deny our God-given need for companionship—to deny that we are dependent on God and to deny that we need one another in order to be the kind of human beings God intended. When we declare that we can make it on our own; when we sing with pride, "I did it my way"; when we turn relationships on and off like a water faucet, according to our thirst, then we not only behave selfishly but we also deny a fundamental aspect of the Christian world view. It ought to make us cry in sorrow and repentance—for our sin, for our heresy, and for our heretical age.

BIBLICAL RELATIONSHIPS

And after the tears, what? We live in a world permeated with the values of individualism. How do we avoid being caught up in them? For that matter, how does Peter Peasant avoid the problem of communalism? If these social forces are so ingrained in our society—if communalism and individualism are so much a part of the warp and woof of their respective social environments—is there any hope for the development of relationships based on a biblical understanding of reality?

Absolutely. But it will not take place if we simply genuflect, confess, and continue on our way. It will happen only if we make a concerted effort (that is, an effort "in concert") to change our approach to relationships—conceptually and behaviorally. The issue of behavioral change will be discussed in subsequent chapters, but for now we must come to terms with the nature and import of the conceptual task. How should the Christian conceive of relationships? And how can we maintain that conception from day to day in a world that is clearly hostile to its presuppositions? Let me suggest three relational principles (or guidelines) that may keep us from steering off course as we attempt to relate to one another as fellow image bearers of God.

1. *Relationships are inherently valuable.* Always before us must remain the fact that God created us as relating beings. He designed us to be in relationships, he expects us to be involved in such relationships, and we need relationships to be fully what God desires. This may sound redundant, but it is absolutely crucial.

We live in a culture that bombards us with an anti-

thetical message. It tells us that relationships are for
our pleasure and that any dependence on them is a
sure sign of human frailty. At the very least, we are
told, we ought never to find ourselves in the position
of "needing" someone else.

But our culture is wrong—fundamentally and essentially wrong. Admitting to the fact that we need one
another is no more an admission of weakness than
admitting to our need for food. To do otherwise is not
bravery, it is stupidity. Together we were created; together we must remain. Relationships, we must continually remind ourselves, are inherently valuable.

2. *Relationships are never an excuse for injustice.* It
seems that human beings have an uncanny ability to
take whatever is worthy and turn it into a thing of
evil. Indeed, one might argue that the greater the object's value, the greater will be its perversion. Surely,
such is the case with human relationships. For just as
the union of two bodies can be bartered for profit, so
established relationships can be used to perpetrate injustice.

The tragedy of such arrangements is that the victims
always seem to be the ones who are attempting to
honor legitimate relationships. The child honoring the
relationship with the parent is the one who risks parental abuse (and vice versa), just as it is the em-
ployee honoring the relationship with the employer
who risks exploitation (and vice versa).

All the persons involved must remember that using
a relationship as an excuse to practice malevolence is
not only wrong, it is a clear subversion of the relationship itself. It is the one legitimate justification for
its termination and, therefore, represents the single
greatest threat to the long-term development of biblical relationships. For the perpetrator, this means that
with the malevolence comes a loss of relational legitimacy (as well as excuse). For the victim, it means a

recognition that the relationship can be honored not only by forbearance but also through an effort to correct the injustice (which might even include the dissolution of the relationship).

Most importantly, for the community, this principle entails an obligation of involvement: the community must intercede on behalf of justice, for the sake of both the victim and the veracity of the relationship itself. It is precisely when the community fails to take corrective action that either the victim is left stranded in unjust relationships (the problem of communalism) or traditional relationships themselves come to be viewed as accessories to the crime (as is the case in individualistic societies). To keep either of these options from happening, the Christian community must act as a community. And its inhabitants must constantly remind themselves that relationships are never an excuse for injustice.

3. *Relationships are not merely a matter of choice.* The most difficult thing for us modern people to appreciate, however, is not the need for justice but the requirement of restraint. It is the seduction of choice that moves our hearts and opens our wallets, and its lure in the area of relationships, as in all other areas, is hard to resist. We *want* to have an enchanting spouse. We *want* a dynamic minister. We *want* to have enviable neighbors. We *want* to have relationships that are satisfying, enjoyable, exciting, and fun.

There is, of course, nothing wrong with stimulating relationships; indeed, they bring great joy into our lives. Nevertheless, although we may choose relationships with the hope that they will have these qualities, many (most?) do not live up to our expectations. The question then becomes: What do we do with unexceptional relationships? The modern answer (the modern necessity) is to trade them in for new ones. Relationships that do not fulfill us are to be discarded in favor of novel possibilities. Such a response is based, first of all, on a hope—a hope that next time we will be able to make a better choice and that next time we will discover a relationship as exciting as the promises of the modern world. Second, it is based on an assumed entitlement—the right to extricate ourselves from relationships that we consider difficult or painful.

The Christian must realize, once again, that the modern approach to relationships is fundamentally wrong. While the desire for satisfying relationships is certainly proper (and good), the hope for a better (alternative) relationship is a vain hope and the right to dissolve troublesome relationships is a bogus right.

We must rid ourselves of the notion that relationships are "things" to be selected and rejected at our convenience. Some relationships are chosen, to be sure, though many are forced on us. Whether or not they are selected, the important thing to remember is that, once we are a part of a relationship, we have a responsibility to see it through. Obviously, "seeing it through" means something different in a friendship than it does, for example, in a marriage. But regardless of the context, it means that we are obligated to relate to other human beings as creatures made in the image of God (not as things)—people who need to be related to us, just as we need to be related to them.

Such an obligation makes the hopes attendant on a new and different relationship irrelevant, and it makes the right to a relationship free from pain absurd. Our duty is to love one another. Our right is to relate to one another. And our hope is to bring the redemption of Christ into the vortex of the relationships that God has given us.

nine / Tradition

When we shift our attention from relationships to traditions, we move to a beast of another color. Not that
the two are unrelated, certainly, since traditions have
much to do with the quality and durability of human
relationships. But from the modern perspective, relationships are at least desirable (provided they are voluntary and self-fulfilling). Traditions, on the other
hand, are hardly even attractive to the modern eye. At
best, they are irrelevant; at worst, impediments to the
good life. To make inquiry into the biblical picture of
traditions in the latter part of the twentieth century,
therefore, is to provoke an indifferent yawn.

But it should not. For there is much to learn from a survey of Scripture concerning the proper role of tradition in the life of the community. Indeed, the problem with such a survey is not in finding something related to the topic but in making a proper judgment as to which passages of Scripture to emphasize and which (for the moment) to set aside. Since my objective is not a thorough exegetical study, however, I will attempt only to specify the recurring themes in Scripture and come to a determination concerning their meaning and implications for us as Christians in the modern world.

Tradition As a Problem

One theme that emerges from any reading of the biblical record seems to be rather critical of the use and abuse of traditions within the religious community. Even a cursory reading of the Gospels, for example, reveals that Christ was willing to break the traditions of his day in order to teach and perform good works. He healed the sick on the Sabbath (Mark 3:1–6). He picked grain for nourishment on the Sabbath (2:23). His disciples did not fast, as John's did (2:18–19), nor did they always properly purify (wash) their hands before they ate (7:2). These lapses in tradition, moreover, were precisely the matters that so irked the Pharisees about Jesus' behavior (or, thus they said). From their perspective, Jesus was not appropriately attentive to the details of their religious tradition. He was a troublemaker, a tradition breaker.

Not only did Jesus break religious traditions (as interpreted by the Pharisees), but he also reserved some of his harshest criticisms for those who were the keepers of tradition. It is to the Pharisees and scribes—those who were extremely careful in their knowledge and execution of every detail of the law and Jewish tradition—that Christ brings the full force of his wrath and condemnation: "Woe to you, teachers of the law and Pharisees, you hypocrites! You give a tenth of your spices—mint, dill and cummin. But you have neglected the more important matters of the law, justice, mercy and faithfulness" (Matthew 23:23). "Woe to you, teachers of the law and Pharisees, you hypocrites! You are like whitewashed tombs, which look beautiful on the outside but on the inside are full of dead men's bones and everything unclean" (v. 27). Of the Pharisees and their traditions, Jesus says, "They tie up heavy loads and put them on men's shoulders" (v. 4). He flatly accused them of preferring the traditions of men to the commandments of God (Matthew 15:2; Mark 7:8). It was a preference about which Christ was not altogether pleased.

Critical comments about empty traditions are not limited to the words of Christ, however. In fact, one might say that Jesus inherited his distaste for hypocrites from his Father. There are few more stinging rebukes of meaningless ritual than those found in the first chapter of Isaiah. There, through his prophet, God says:

> "The multitude of your sacrifices—
>   what are they to me?" says the Lord;
> I have more than enough of burnt offerings,
>   of rams and the fat of fattened animals;
> I have no pleasure
>   in the blood of bulls and lambs and goats.
> When you come to meet with me,
>   who has asked this of you,
>   this trampling of my courts?
> Stop bringing meaningless offerings!
>   Your incense is detestable to me.
> New Moons, Sabbaths and convocations—
>   I cannot bear your evil assemblies.
> Your New Moon festivals and your appointed
>   feasts my soul hates.

> They have become a burden to me;
>   I am weary of bearing them.
> When you spread out your hands in prayer,
>   I will hide my eyes from you;
> even if you offer many prayers,
>   I will not listen.
> Your hands are full of blood."
>
> Isaiah 1:11-15

In these verses, as in others, a critical theme concerning traditions is clear and unambiguous. It starkly reminds us that traditions can be used as barriers to good works. They can also be used to promote human pride and to mask a sinful heart. Under such conditions, God is not pleased with traditions. In fact, they are an abomination to him—"meaningless offerings" that his "soul hates."

Tradition As a Gift

But there is an older theme in Scripture than the critical one. It begins with the creation of an evaluating being and finds its expression throughout the Bible. It is a story about a God who acts in history and desires that his people remember his actions. It is a story about a God who wants his people to show their love for him through obedience to his laws and love for their neighbors. It is the story of a God who expects his children to honor his ways as they honor the ways of their parents. It is a God deeply concerned about tradition.

I was first struck by this second theme on my initial "leisurely" reading of Exodus (which did not happen until I was in my twenties, unfortunately; before that, I was always reading for study and/or speed). As I made my way through the Red Sea crossing, the murmuring of the Israelites, the manna from God, the establishment of the covenant, and the giving of the law, I was suddenly (massively) confronted by God's detailed prescriptions to Moses concerning the presentation of an appropriate offering and the building of the tabernacle. Beginning with chapter 25, one reads page after page of intricate orders concerning the construction of the ark, the table, the lampstand, the curtain, the altar, the courts, and the tabernacle itself, after which comes a description of the service, including a discussion of the priest's garments, ordination, use of incense, etc. Apparently, God was not content with just "any old" ceremony. He wanted a specific kind of service, full of meaningful detail and rich symbolism. He wanted to establish a tradition that was worthy of the event it represented.

How odd all of this seemed to me as I paced myself through the remaining chapters of Exodus. After all, had not God read the future accurately? Did he not know that his people would abuse his traditions? That priests would cleverly obey every detail of the tradition while forgetting about its real meaning? Couldn't he foresee that celebrants would carry through with the ritual, regardless of the intent of their hearts, and even gain a false sense of security through doing what was prescribed? Did he not know, after all, that ultimately devotion is a thing of faith, not of offerings and sacrifices? Good grief, had he not been able to foretell the words of his own prophets and even his only Son?

And yet, there is more. Much more. Not only do we discover that God makes a rather "big deal" out of maintaining the Sabbath tradition (Leviticus 19:30)—had he not anticipated Christ's words and deeds?—but he even has Isaiah (of *all* people!) proclaiming (in chapter 56) that those who keep the Sabbath will be blessed!

But possibly the most incredible episode of all is described in 1 Chronicles 13. For here is the story of Uzzah, a man who happened to be driving the cart that was carrying the ark from Kiriath Jearim to Jerusalem by order of King David and the assembly of Israel. It was a happy occasion, and "David and all the Israelites were celebrating with all their might before God" (v. 8). When the cart reached "the threshing floor of Kidon," however, one of the oxen pulling the cart stumbled. Uzzah, concerned that the ark might fall, "reached out his hand to steady the ark." In response, "the LORD's anger burned against Uzzah, and he struck him down because he had put his hand on the ark. So he died there before God" (v. 10).

Now why would God do such a thing? There is no indication that Uzzah did anything intentionally wrong, nor that his heart was evil or his actions poorly motivated. Quite the contrary. Uzzah seemed to be engaging in an altruistic act. What we do know, however, is that the ark should not have been carried by an ox and cart, but by Levites using "poles of acacia wood" (Exodus 25:13). In other words, the details of God's instructions were not being fulfilled. Thus, despite Uzzah's seemingly unwitting position, God became angry, and Uzzah paid the price. And, once again, we are left to ask God, "Why?" Why this concern for the details of tradition when all that matters is the heart? Why, to be specific, should God take out his vengeance on a man whose heart seemed to be in the right place even though his actions were not quite proper?

Nor do we have to confine ourselves to the Old Testament to find evidence of God's concern for tradition. Christ himself, though characterized by the Pharisees as a tradition breaker, warned: "Do not think that I have come to abolish the Law or the Prophets; I have come not to abolish them but to fulfill them. I tell you the truth, until heaven and earth disappear, not the smallest letter, not the least stroke of a pen, will by any means disappear from the Law until everything is accomplished" (Matthew 5:17–18).

146

Though some modern people might wish to differenti-
ate between the law and tradition at this point, one
suspects that the audience listening with the Hebrew
mind would not have done so, nor would the Hebrew
making the statement.

It is interesting to note, moreover, that the one incident of physical anger displayed by Christ occurred
because of the misuse of temple tradition. Thus, after
his triumphal entry into Jerusalem, Jesus went to the
temple and "began driving out those who were buying
and selling there . . . . And as he taught them, he said,
'Is it not written:

> " 'My house shall be called
> a house of prayer for all nations'?

But you have made it 'a den of robbers'" (Mark 11:15,
17). From the modern perspective, however, one
rather wonders why Jesus was so perturbed. After all,
the temple is just an edifice, is it not? We, not the
building, are the temple of the Holy Spirit. So why
unduly fret oneself about the misuse of a mere symbol?

WHY DOES GOD CARE?

To the modern ear, filled with the music of individualism, the questions we pose do sound peculiar. Indeed, from the modern perspective, Christ *did* over-
react a bit at the temple. And God *did* lay it on a
little thick with the acacia wood, cubits, rings, and all
("Make a curtain of blue, purple and scarlet yarn and
finely twisted linen; with cherubim worked into it by
a skilled craftsman. Hang it with gold hooks on four
posts of acacia wood overlaid with gold and standing
on four silver bases" [Exodus 26:31–32]). And in the
case of Uzzah—well, one rather suspects that the Lord
completely lost his sense of fair play in that affair (or,
if one comes out of a less literal subculture, that pos-

sibly Uzzah tripped on a rock and died of a concussion, the people ignorantly attributing it to an act of God). In any case, the modern mind simply has no way of coping with these events—aside from excusing them, forgetting them, or demythologizing them. It's all much too vulgar to think about seriously.

For those primitive souls who remain willing to take Holy Scripture seriously, however, these incidents remind us of at least this, that God cares about his traditions. He cares about them, first of all, because he takes his word seriously. When he tells someone that the ark ought to be two cubits by two-and-a-half cubits by two-and-a-half cubits, then the ark jolly well better be built just that way. God expects his people to honor his instructions (and that accounts, in part I think, for the death of Uzzah and Christ's anger in the temple).

However, God obviously believes that traditions serve a purpose beyond sheer obedience. He did not establish them simply so he could one day zap Uzzah in a rather idiosyncratic manner or trip up the Pharisees. Rather, he crafted his traditions, in all their detail and splendor for the benefit (and again I say *benefit*) of his people. Traditions are *for* us, not against us. They remind us of events that need to be remembered, experiences that ought to be symbolized, joys that crave to be rekindled, sorrows that yearn to be borne again. We need them because we are finite—we forget what God has done for us; we misplace the date of a child's birth; we lose the meaning of a marriage vow. We need them because we are fallible—we sometimes prefer to neglect God's love, or love's promise, or a parent's responsibility. We need them because a life empty of tradition is a life void of its past and incapable of producing a meaningful future. It is a life of impoverished freedom.

In this light, the "critical theme" discussed earlier

takes on a different hue. It is not, as some moderns would have us believe, the new message of the Gospels, but a restoration of a very old one. It tells us, in the strongest possible language, that God's traditions are too valuable to be abused, too meaningful to be demeaned. When God rails against sacrifices and offerings (in Isaiah 1), it is not the traditions that he hates, but the iniquity of a people whose "hands are full of blood" (v. 15). When Jesus rebukes the Pharisees for their hypocrisy, it is not their tradition keeping that he despises, but the emptiness of their actions ("So you must obey them and do everything they tell you. But do not do what they do, for they do not practice what they preach" (Matthew 23:3). Sanity, as well as logic, precludes our using such biblical texts to justify the disparagement of tradition. They are, rather, a clarion call for traditions with purpose and significance. From them we learn that traditions used to cover up evil are counterfeit; they can neither bring about the desired outcome for the participant nor the blessings of God. It is because the genuine article is so precious that its fabrication is so vile.

When Jesus' disciples were accused of breaking tradition by plucking grain on the Sabbath, Jesus responded to his interrogators (after a brief history lesson) with these words: "The Sabbath was made for man, not man for the Sabbath. So the Son of Man is Lord even of the Sabbath" (Mark 2:27–28). The modern mind seems to interpret these words as a justification for dispensing with tradition. It's as if Christ suddenly gave his disciples the right to practice the Sabbath in any way they chose. That interpretation is intriguing, certainly, but believable only in the modern era (and thus *not* believed by preceding generations). A much more straightforward reading would suggest that (1) Christ is Lord of the Sabbath; (2) he made the Sabbath for blokes just like you and me;

and (3) the Sabbath commandment was established for the benefit of humanity, not for its depravation. Thus if one is hungry, one ought not feel that plucking a bit of grain is an encroachment on the law. As far as I can tell, the modern notion—that man is lord of the Sabbath—is the one conclusion explicitly ruled out by the words of Christ.

TRADITION AND HYPOCRISY

And still the modern mind persists: Don't traditions breed hypocrisy? Is it not inevitable that people will, after a time, engage in them "ritualistically" (note, parenthetically, the modern connotation of that term), discarding their intent, and using them to flaunt their religiosity? Would it not be preferable simply to dispense with traditions altogether and concentrate instead on the "essence" of the experience? Is not tradition a crutch that does more harm than good?

It is true, of course, that traditions breed hypocrisy—in the same way that rules breed deviance. There is not a doubt in the world that once a norm is established, someone will violate it. And just as surely, a tradition, once in place, will be performed meaninglessly. But few there are who wish to terminate all forms of law in order to eradicate deviance. Why, then, do we wish to liquidate traditions in order to cure all forms of hypocrisy?

Why, indeed? Peter Peasant would not have known why. His world was ripe with both tradition and hypocrisy, but he would not have dreamed someone would actually eliminate traditions in order to guard against hypocrisy. Only Martin Modern would use such logic. But then, one suspects it is not logic that Martin finds so compelling.

Are All Traditions Valuable?

And yet the questions come. Let us assume that some traditions are important—those explicitly instituted by God, for example. Is it therefore true that all traditions are valuable? Are not some traditions, in fact, quite despicable? And if some are worthy while others are not, how does one discern the difference? In short, has a case been made for the value of tradition in general, or merely of biblical traditions in particular?

Admittedly, these are difficult questions. In some ways, a case has not been made for anything, as the argument here is more of a plea for tolerance than a legal brief. I must confess, as well, that at this point in our history I would be overjoyed if "merely biblical traditions" were taken seriously. Nevertheless, all of this begs the question. What I do believe is that the Bible presents God as a Being deeply concerned with human traditions. He is a God who creates them (in the most lavish forms imaginable), guards them, and despises those who abuse them and use them for their own selfish ends. He obviously believes that his traditions are good for us, that we need them, and that we will be a more robust people if we cherish them.

It is also my firm conviction that God knew what he was doing when he established specific traditions for the people of Israel. In spite of opening up the possibility of hypocrisy and abuse, traditions are valuable and necessary to the human community, enabling us to remember things that ought to be remembered and to solidify relationships that ought to be solidified. When traditions allow us to worship God and to remember his actions in our lives and history, they are valuable. When traditions enable us to honor our parents, set aside a day for rest and worship, confess our sins, or love our God, then they are valuable. When traditions encourage us to pursue truth and value the Truth that we have, then they are valuable. When traditions help us to remember our history and the history of the human race, then they are valuable. When traditions bring us together and hold us in relationships that are durable and long-lasting, then they are valuable.

But clearly, some traditions do none of these things. Some traditions may pervert relationships and lead us to worship false gods. It is one of the great ironies of our age, in fact, that although we live in an era of traditionlessness, the few rituals in which we manage to participate are either encumbrances to virtue or, in some cases, patently idolatrous. Our "traditions" (and one winces to call them such) involve mute evenings around a flashing inanimate object, or purposeless ventures among faceless crowds. Moreover, church history suggests that Christians have sometimes developed religious traditions that are not only extrabiblical but also nonbiblical. In such circumstances, traditions may be set above, used against, or put in competition with Scripture. When this happens—when traditions pervert God's justice, his order, or his Word—they are anathema. With the God of Isaiah, we must rail against them. In any age and in any era, good traditions can be abused and poor traditions can be developed—as can laws, and relationships, and any other good gift given by God to his creatures.

The question is, are these reasons to abandon tradition altogether? The modern assumption seems to be, "Yes; traditions are innocuous at best, and more than likely dangerous." It is an attitude that presumes that traditions are frivolous and trifling unless proven otherwise. But, surely, such an assumption is not Christian, is it?

I am willing to say no. Traditions should not be

dropped at the first sign of hypocrisy nor live under a cloud of suspicion. A tradition attempting to operate under the presupposition of guilt is not long a tradition, for its life depends on value and its sustenance requires respect. It is far preferable, I believe, to suppose that a tradition is worthy until proven otherwise. I say this, not merely because I think traditions are inherently valuable (which I do), but because traditions in the modern world are like palm trees in a desert. It may be that some should be cut down, but there jolly well better be a good reason for it.

ten / Vision

And then there is vision—the single remaining element of community, whose importance few Christians would wish to deny. It is vision that takes us beyond ourselves, putting our lives in the context of eternity, thus making the act of community possible. It is vision toward which tradition should point us, and it is vision that ought to motivate us to build enduring relationships. For the Christian community, therefore, one would think vision should be in abundant supply. After all, Christians believe in God; Christians believe that he is the Creator of heaven and earth and that we are the products of his hand. Christians are "the believers," we sometimes hear, even in an age of skepticism and doubt. Of vision, Christians have a well-stocked storehouse.

True enough. Beliefs we have in great quantity in the modern church. Indeed, we have elevated beliefs to center stage in most of our congregations—honing them, shaping them, and modifying them to meet the demands of twentieth-century living. And thus our difficulty. For the problem with the modern Christian vision is not that it lacks a transcendent element but that it accommodates its purview so thoroughly to the needs of the social setting.

An Accommodated Vision

Remember that Peter Peasant's problem with vision was that he felt fatalistic about life. It appeared to him that his world was created and defined for him by the authority of external agents and powers. For the Christian in such circumstances, it often seems as if God is simply one more (or *the*) imposing figure in his or her life. God is the Mastermind behind one's fate and he is the Power who determines one's destiny in life. He gives noble blood to some—they are one's rulers; he gives the common touch to others— they are one's neighbors. In any case, from Peter's perspective, Peter is relatively powerless to change his environment or his place within that environment. Because of this vision of fatalism, he easily can become the victim of communalism. All that needs to happen is for God's will to be fused with the will of the community, and Peter's fate is sealed.

Martin Modern's problem, on the other hand—*our* problem, more accurately—is that we behave as if everything is up to us. It is as if we are the only decision makers of consequence; as if we are the molders of our destiny. This does *not* mean that we do not sometimes feel like the victims of forces beyond our control. Indeed, we do. Moderns are quite disposed to feel victimized by biology or society or dumb luck (i.e., random distribution of events). However, this is "meaningless" victimization, not something that fits into the grand plans of transcendent beings. The point is, for Martin Modern, human decisions are the only variables of consequence; they are the things on which he must always depend.

For the Christian in the modern world, then, there is a strong temptation to ignore the Reality to which one theoretically subscribes. By that I mean that the modern Christian is inclined to *talk* about God, but to ignore the implications of such talk in everyday life. I am continually amazed at how the most pious of modern Christians can talk continuously about "God's will," "God's grace," and "God's sovereignty," and in the midst of such verbiage make decisions (in the church and everywhere else) based purely on the modern values of individualism, efficiency, self-interest, and consumerism. It is as if there is no recognition at all that one's verbal expressions draw on a vision that is significantly in conflict with the vision that gives rise to one's actions. What this means is that we modern Christians, regardless of how orthodox we may appear, often behave as products of the modern vision (which, in large part, we are) rather than as a people rooted in a Christian world view.

A Christian Vision

The question before us, then, is what should our vision of God's worldly involvement look like? Peter Peasant makes God out to be an ogre, a Greek deity manipulating the tragedies of life. Martin Modern, on the other hand, makes him out to be a hermit or a recluse—a disinterested bystander in the affairs of humanity. But how should we think about this Being we call God? And what is his relationship with the people of the earth?

These may seem to be gigantic questions, far beyond the scope of a book like this. But though these questions loom large before us, I am convinced their answers are not difficult to find. What gives us trouble, in fact, is not discerning them, but fully comprehending and applying them. It is in the understanding that we fail, not in dogma.

Two biblical insights, it would seem, are especially salient to any understanding of God's relationship with humanity. First is the fact that he is our Creator. "And the LORD God formed man from the dust of the the ground and breathed into his nostrils the breath of life, and man became a living being" (Genesis 2:7). This fact is well known to us. We see its truth repeated numerous times throughout Scripture, and we hear it from the pulpit, in sermons and prayers alike, at regular intervals. Such repetition is appropriate, in my opinion. It is a crucial assumption about the nature of the Person we call God.

The other important aspect of this relationship is that, in his sovereign will, God created us with the ability to make choices about our destiny. In the garden, of course, that choice was comparatively simple. "Then God said, 'I give you every seed-bearing plant on the face of the whole earth and every tree that has fruit with seed in it. They will be yours for food'" (Genesis 1:29). "You are free to eat from any tree in the garden; but you must not eat from the tree of the knowledge of good and evil" (Genesis 2:16–17). Thus God gave Adam and Eve the capacity to disobey him—to make a choice that would radically affect their future. When they chose to disobey God, that decision did not abrogate their decision-making ability, but it did make future choices much more difficult and complicated. Not only would the environment for future choices be a more hostile one (Genesis 3:16–19), but they would have to be made in the

context of an expanded knowledge base: "The man
has become like one of us, knowing good and evil"
(Genesis 3:22). Although I will (gladly) let other scholars discover all the facets of that little gem, I must
point out the obvious conclusion that the Fall did not
make the human being *less* of a choosing being, but
more of one. That is, the possibilities of disobedience
became expanded a millionfold with the introduction
of sin. Nevertheless, though making choices is more
difficult, we still have the possibility of choosing obedience after the Fall.

These two facts—that we were created by a gracious
God and that we can, in the context of his sovereignty, make choices about our destiny—are central to a
Christian vision of humanity's relationship to God. Unfortunately, however, they are two facts not easily remembered by Christians in everyday life. I suspect
that there are many reasons for such lapses of mem-
ory, but one seems particularly important: these two
facts come to us, both in theory and practice, as a bit
of a paradox. The first signifies dependence, whereas
the second implies independence; the first suggests
the need for trust, whereas the second indicates the
possibility of self-reliance; the first provokes thoughts
of God's sovereignty, whereas the second engenders
the notion of human autonomy; the first inclines us to
think of God's greatness and the second, of man's.
This last paradox seems to be captured by David:

O Lord, our Lord,
how majestic is your name in all the earth!

You have set your glory
   above the heavens.
From the lips of children and infants
   you have ordained praise
because of your enemies,
   to silence the foe and the avenger.

When I consider your heavens,
    the work of your fingers,
the moon and the stars,
    which you have set in place,
what is man that you are mindful of him,
    the son of man that you care for him?
You made him a little lower than the heavenly beings
    and crowned him with glory and honor,

You have made him ruler over the works of your hands;
    you put everything under his feet:
all flocks and herds,
    and the beasts of the field,
the birds of the air,
    and the fish of the sea,
    all that swim the paths of the seas.

O Lord, our Lord,
    how majestic is your name in all the earth!"

                                                Psalm 8

Sadly, the conclusion, "How majestic is your name!" reached by the psalmist pondering this paradox has not been the one reached by all Christians over the years. Indeed, I believe that the single greatest problem with the Christian vision of community is its tendency to emphasize one of these two truths at the expense of the other. For Peter Peasant, the problem tended to be the fact of his dependence on God; for Martin Modern, it is the existence of human freedom.

The telling point—the thing that ought to catch our attention—is that in choosing one biblical truth over the other, Peter and Martin are selecting a theology to suit their social circumstances. Peter, or more accurately, the church during Peter's era, emphasized the need for human dependence and submission precisely at the time that the society was characterized by immobility, status ascription, and inflexible lines of authority. Martin, on the other hand, hears the church rave about possibility thinking and the glories of human achievement precisely when his society is characterized by social mobility, status achievement, and the breakdown of traditional authority. While it is not at all clear whether the church is shaping society or the society is shaping the church, one thing is certain: Christians, in both settings, are getting a half-baked vision of ultimate reality, and the half they are getting is exactly the one they already have in excess.

To have a Christian vision consistent with biblical truths and appropriate to the needs of genuine community (and I consider the two synonymous), we must not be satisfied with a half-baked view of our relationship with God. For us in the modern world this means we must assert that (and *live* as if) God is our Creator. It means that we must appreciate every day as a gift from God, every creature as the yield of God's artistry, and every choice before us as an opportunity to be obedient to our Creator.

CONCLUSION

Indeed, it is in our approach to choices that we confront the fundamental challenge of modernity. We can view them, like the world around us, as a right to be exercised and a mechanism of self-fulfillment; but in so doing, we will liquidate the possibility of Christian community. The other option is to view our decision-making ability as God's image within us, a precious and risky gift from the Creator to those whom he loves. To choose to love him back—to choose to use this gift to honor and obey the Giver—is to choose the only road that can lead us to a proper life together. It is the starting point for those who wish to build genuine community in the midst of modernity.

PART V / The Faithful Community

eleven / **Affirming the Vision of the Faithful**

So what shall we do? Those of us who believe that *relationships* are given to us by God, for our good and our necessity, and are inherently valuable; those who understand that *traditions* are not impediments to meaningful living, but helpful guides from the beacon events of our past into future unknowns; those who profess that a Christian *vision* includes both the fact of our createdness and the fact that we were created to make responsible choices—what shall we do? How can we take these beliefs, understandings, and professions from the nod of an assent toward the reality of a Christian life together?

One thing is certain: we cannot do it with a ten-point plan on how to build a religious community. Such an approach would be self-defeating. And this must be the first lesson for those wishing to establish a faithful community: to dash off quickly and attempt the development of techniques for building religious community is to let the values of modernity dictate the solution to the problem. It is something like responding to the itch of a rash by scratching: although it may be momentarily satisfying, its long-term effect is to spread the infection. If we are to work toward the establishment of Christian communities, we must begin—not with techniques, or means, or "how to" strategies—but by affirming the vision of the faithful community.

STARTING WITH VALUES

To begin this discussion with a plea for correct vision might seem a rather odd thing to do. After all, a vision is the product of certain values, and a common assumption in modern social science is that values reflect their environment. Therefore, if one wants to change values, one ought first to create a different environment. There is, moreover, good reason for such an assumption. Often, human beings appear to express values that conveniently "fit" their social circumstances. Indeed, much of the argument made thus far hinges on the idea that the social arrangements of modernity have reordered our values, making genuine community difficult if not impossible. Clearly, human values are significantly influenced by social conditions—sometimes for better, but often for worse.

Nevertheless, Christians must not allow this tendency to be taken as an unalterable fact. Just as we know that the social setting affects our values, we must also hold fast to the similarly biblical principle that we can select values and attempt to fashion our environment on that basis. We are neither free of our social circumstances nor entirely trapped by them. We can, as God's image bearers, make choices about such things as values, beliefs, and world views, and these choices will, if we allow them, hold sway over our lives. We can, in short, develop a vision. But this ability to choose aspects of our own vision is not, as modernity claims, the result of our status as demigods, but the fact that God has created us with the possibility of making such decisions, as well as with the responsibility to make good decisions. It is to the task of making such "good decisions" that we now turn.

AN ANCIENT TRUTH

What sort of vision is it that will sustain the Christian community? It is the same vision that has sustained the church since its inception. It is rooted, first of all, in a common understanding of what we believe. And it is driven, secondly, by a common aspiration concerning how we ought to function. The first we will term an *ancient truth;* the second, an *enduring ideal.*

The Christian community has always been grounded in orthodoxy. It is a community based on truth. It is not a response to desire. It is not a projection of our needs. It is not the result of our hopes. It is not a reaction to our fears. The Christian community derives its being from the fact that certain things are true. If they are not true, we have no reason for community. If they are true, we have no alternative but to unite around them. These truths have always been, and will always be, the source of our togetherness and our belonging.

About these core truths we have not been left to speculate. They are clearly presented in Holy Scripture, and the early church fathers carefully preserved them in a wide variety of creeds and forms. The

167

Niceno-Constantinopolitan Creed, for example, renders them in the following manner:

> I believe in one God the Father Almighty, maker of heaven and earth, and of all things visible and invisible: And in one Lord Jesus Christ, the only-begotten Son of God, begotten of His Father before all worlds, God of God, Light of Light, very God of very God, begotten, not made, being of one substance with the Father, by whom all things were made; Who for us men and for our salvation came down from heaven, and was incarnate by the Holy Spirit of the Virgin Mary, and was made man, and crucified also for us under Pontius Pilate; He suffered and was buried, and the third day He rose again according to the Scriptures, and ascended into heaven, and sitteth on the right hand of the Father; And He shall come again with glory to judge both the quick and the dead; Whose kingdom shall have no end.
>
> And I believe in the Holy Spirit, the Lord and giver of life, who proceedeth from the Father and the Son, who with the Father and the Son together is worshipped and glorified; who spoke by the prophets.
>
> And I believe in one universal and apostolic church; I acknowledge one baptism for the remission of sins, and I look for the resurrection of the dead, and the life of the world to come. Amen.

Amen, indeed. You see, we need no novel truths to create a religious community. Nor do we need new insight into the mind of God, nor an exceptional personage to guide us into uncharted waters. In fact, the search for a novel vision that "will work" fundamentally obstructs community building. At best, it obscures the historical nature of the task. At worst, it leads to all kinds of heretical and cultic communal efforts. We need, instead, to affirm the vision of the ancients—to commit ourselves to that which we already know or, more likely, to rediscover what it is that has been salient for Christians over the years.

The question is, Do we believe the vision handed down to us by the historical Christian church—not in the modern sense of rational assent, but in the life-changing sense of the biblical record? Do we deeply and unabashedly believe the truths of the Christian faith? More importantly, do we believe them enough to base our actions on them? That, in the modern world, is the crux of the matter. We live in a world of facile belief. It is easy for us to replace, rebuke, or retrofit our beliefs as the occasion demands. But we will not be willing or able to go against the grain of modernity unless the vision we hold is capable of promoting consistent behavior.

Those wishing to work toward the development of Christian community, therefore, must begin by asking themselves whether or not they have a passion for the "old, old story." If so, they have begun their trek toward the desired destination. If not, they haven't a chance of reaching it, regardless of good intentions. Indeed, the road paved with good intentions points in a rather different direction.

An Enduring Ideal

If founded on the rock of an ancient truth, the Christian community is built according to the specifications of a truly grand design. It is a design often presented in Holy Scripture but seldom realized in the life of the local church. But before we investigate the problem of implementation, let us appreciate, once again, the beauty of the Master's plan as given in 1 Corinthians 12:4–27:

> There are different kinds of gifts, but the same Spirit. There are different kinds of service, but the same Lord. There are different kinds of working, but the same God works all of them in all men.

169

Now to each one the manifestation of the Spirit is given for the common good. To one there is given through the Spirit the message of wisdom, to another the message of knowledge by means of the same Spirit, to another faith by the same Spirit, to another gifts of healing by that one Spirit, to another miraculous powers, to another prophecy, to another the ability to distinguish between spirits, to another the ability to speak in different kinds of tongues, and to still another the interpretation of tongues. All these are the work of one and the same Spirit, and he gives them to each one, just as he determines.

The body is a unit, though it is made up of many parts; and though all its parts are many, they form one body. So it is with Christ. For we were all baptized by one Spirit into one body—whether Jews or Greeks, slave or free—and we were all given the one Spirit to drink.

Now the body is not made up of one part but of many. If the foot should say, "Because I am not a hand, I do not belong to the body," it would not for that reason cease to be part of the body. And if the ear should say, "Because I am not an eye, I do not belong to the body," it would not for that reason cease to be part of the body. If the whole body were an eye, where would the sense of hearing be? If the whole body were an ear, where would the sense of smell be? But in fact God has arranged the parts in the body, every one of them, just as he wanted them to be. If they were all one part, where would the body be? As it is, there are many parts, but one body.

The eye cannot say to the hand, "I don't need you!" And the head cannot say to the feet, "I don't need you!" On the contrary, those parts of the body that seem to be weaker are indispensable, and the parts that we think are less honorable we treat with special honor. And the parts that are unpresentable are treated with special modesty, while our presentable parts need no special treatment. But God has combined the members of the body and has given greater honor to the parts that lacked it, so that there should be no division in the body, but that its parts should have equal concern for each other. If one part suffers, every part suffers with it; if one part is honored, every part rejoices with it.

Now you are the body of Christ, and each one of you is a part of it.

Strange as it may seem, when I read these words, I am reminded of an Amish barn. The reason for this odd association is that the Amish build their barns together. When a family is in need of a barn (or almost anything else, for that matter), the people of the community join in a common effort to construct it for them. Nothing about this effort, however, is done haphazardly or without forethought. Everyone has a role to perform, a task to accomplish. The project is carefully planned and executed with a good deal of energy and vigor. Most importantly, the barn is the product of the community. When it is finished, it testifies to the ability of a people to use their diverse gifts in order to accomplish a single purpose.

That is not an insignificant testimony. It has very practical consequences. Imagine for a moment that you are the Amish family for whom the barn has been built. When you awaken in the morning and peer out your window at the barn, what will you see? Not just an object. Not merely a personal possession. But a *gift*. It is something you have because of the sacrifice and investment of others. You will not put an advertisement for "Rosie's Tobacco" on its roof. Nor will you scribble "Smile—God loves you" on its sides or allow it to deteriorate over the years. To abuse the barn in any way would be a denial of its meaning and an insult to the community. In honor of the givers, you will respect and appreciate the gift. You will, in short, be a good steward.

171

Contrast the Amish view of the barn with the modern view of *things*. The things we have are our possessions. They belong to us and we treat them according to our own personal standards. Most importantly, we do not view them as gifts but see them as the product of our own efforts. We go out and get a job, receive a salary, and then use the money to purchase whatever we need or desire. Thus we deserve the things we have (we think) and feel no responsibility to others concerning them.

Of course, this modern view of things is really a fiction, since our possessions also result from the sacrifices of others. The chair I sit on exists because of the labor and imagination of others; so too does my car, my home, and my pencil. I rarely think of these things as gifts, however, because I purchased them myself. Currency, for all its advantages, impersonalizes consumption and veils the link between community and consumer. It enables me to look at my material blessings and say, without apology, "That's mine."

That's too bad. Because the Amish view of the barn is more realistic. It reminds us that our notion of self-sufficiency is a farce and that we are not self-made men and women, obligated only to pursue our own interests. We, as much as the Amish, need one another. Our possessions, along with our pleasures and very survival, are made possible through the efforts of others.

IDEAL MEANINGS

The question is, does our vision for the Christian community resemble the Amish view of the barn or the modern perspective on things? The church, of course, is not an Amish community. Nor, in my opinion, ought it to function as one. Despite my appreciation for the Amish people and their Anabaptist heritage, I do not think the Christian community is called to live a segregated life. Nevertheless, the local church ought to function as a particular expression of the body of Christ. And if I understand the words of the apostle Paul correctly, the body ought to be about the business of building Amish barns, not modern structures.

That means, first of all, recognizing that we are united by a common purpose. We worship one God. We are redeemed by one Savior. And we are given gifts by one Spirit. It is for that purpose that we build our barn. We do not build it for the education committee, the pastor, or anyone else. Nor does the barn we build belong solely to us. The barn is built for the Lord and belongs ultimately to him. Our unity—our barn—stands as a testimony to him. It reminds us that we cannot callously "do our own thing" in the Christian community. We are doing His thing. And it reminds the world of what it so desperately wants to ignore: that Jesus Christ is Lord.

A second consequence of this vision is the recognition that our unity does not come at the expense of diversity. In fact, our diversity is the result of God's own design. The One who unites us has made us diverse so that we might build a truly Grand Barn. This is important. Some of us attempt to maintain our unity by building small barns, knowing that it is easier for our own small group to stay together if everyone works on the same task; out of such thinking, many cults are born. Others want to build gigantic barns, employing a great variety or workers, but they forget why, or for whom, the barn is being built; out of such thinking, many modern churches arise. But we are called neither to build small barns for our leaders nor great barns for ourselves. We are called to be a part of the grandest project of all times—we are called to be the body of Christ.

CONCLUSION

In the final analysis, of course, the biblical picture of the body of Christ is not merely an ideal toward which we ought to strive. It is a living, existential reality of which we are a part. Like the Amish view of the barn, it is the only realistic perspective. No matter how small we may think the barn is, it remains a Grand Barn. Regardless of how unrelated we may feel to other members of the building project, we are knit together by a single Architect. And whether or not we think the barn belongs to us or the choir director or the sexton, it continues to belong to its rightful Owner. The Grand Barn exists. Despite our limited vision of the Christian community, the body of Christ remains.

The question for us, therefore, is not, Will the body of Christ survive the ravishes of modernity? It is, rather, Will the modern Christian community participate in the body of Christ? The answer, I believe, substantially depends on whether or not its vision is rooted in truth and inspired by the Spirit "for the common good."

twelve / Questioning the Judgments of Modern Religion

If a passionate affirmation of the Christian vision is the first step in the development of Christian community, then an equally intense skepticism of modernity is the second. This does not necessarily mean that modern values must be rejected outright or even always resisted. But it does recognize that the spirit of our age is significantly predisposed against the possibility of community. Those who wish to build and sustain Christian communities, therefore, will need to question the judgments of modernity—persistently, carefully, and with a jaundiced eye.

QUESTION: IS RELEVANCE THE PROPER CRITERION?

I noted earlier that in a religious market it is easy to allow relevance to become the key factor in making decisions about everything from educational programs to theology. This is because modern parishioners have a strong desire to attract new members into their particular religious assembly. In order to accomplish this goal, the church becomes increasingly concerned with, and will go to great lengths to make inquiry into, the "wants" of the consumer. On the basis of the religious consumer's response to such inquiries, churches then go about the task of developing programs and theologies that are relevant to the consumer's desires. If the consumer is worried about crime, then one develops a theology of law and order. If the consumer is concerned about the exploitation of the poor in Peru, then one develops a theology of liberation. Whatever the consumer wants, the relevant church is able to deliver.

At the outset, I want to assert that the needs of the congregation are extremely important. A religious community should be in the business of meeting the needs of its parishioners. One way of doing this, moreover, is by asking people what they perceive to be their concerns. Christian compassion and sensitivity suggests that this is a proper approach. Someone who wants to build a Christian community without listening to the trials and tribulations of other community members will surely fail. It would be folly to create a program to meet specific needs without first consulting those whom the program is intended to help. Nothing I have said about questioning the value of relevance precludes the necessity for sensitivity or intelligence.

However, two things should be kept in mind at this point. First, perceived needs are not necessarily accurate (nor necessarily inaccurate) assessments, and, second, there is a difference between relevance and "relatedness."

We have come to the place in social discourse these days where we take as gospel whatever people say about themselves. This tendency is rooted in another modern notion—that "I am the most reliable source of information on myself." I am not immune to this tendency; I am irked beyond reason when my self-assessment is contradicted and I find it equally unbearable for others to tell me how to behave. Such a response, however, is not only an obvious attempt at self-justification on my part, but it is also quite in line with modern assumptions about value relativity and the inapplicability of sin. It presupposes, for one thing, that what I say about myself is my own business (i.e., I can choose my own values as a base from which to evaluate myself) and, for another, that what I say about my character or action should be taken as truth (or as close to truth as modernity can get). The first assumption ignores the Christian idea that values are not all created equal, while the second ignores the fact of sin (or, in this case, self-interest).

What this suggests is that self-assessment of perceived needs is often flawed, both because one may use wrong values to make such assessments and because people often distort the truth (when it hurts) in order to make themselves look good (or more needy, or less needy, or whatever). When we deal with the perceived worries and concerns of others, we must bear in mind that they could be distorted or even wrong. This means that we must listen not only with sympathetic hearts but also with discerning minds. It also means that we ought not to go out and immediately change our theology to meet a particular need (not, that is, without a great deal of prayer and thought). We could be producing a theology for a counterfeit need.

Second, it seems most prudent to distinguish relevance from relatedness. To relate the doctrines of the church to the concerns of modern people is clearly a worthy (and necessary) goal. Theology must be understood to be of value. Thus it must be translated into many languages, not just literally, but in the sense that it must take root in the hearts of people who live in very different circumstances and contexts.

But the need for relatedness is vastly different from the requirement for relevance. The former tries to communicate the truth as it is understood, while the latter is often willing to make the truth adapt to the needs of the audience. The first looks to a tradition of truth for answers to contemporary problems, while the latter looks to contemporary problems to determine the answers. Admittedly, in some situations, the practical line between relating and relevance is ambiguous, especially for those translating truth from one culture to another. But the outcome is substantially different. For while relatedness produces a fresh understanding of the religious tradition (and a higher regard for it), relevance generates a "new" understanding of truth and a not-so-subtle disdain for those "trapped in the ways of the past." The best evidence of motive is still fruit.

It is precisely because the value of relevance always seems to imply change that we must be wary of its influence. Change, of course, is not necessarily a bad thing. Indeed, an effective Christian community will need to be programmatically flexible as well as environmentally adaptive. But changes can also destroy a Christian community, especially when they occur in its core elements—its vision and its traditions. When the value of relevance becomes god, everything else is up for grabs. Changes are no longer merely possible, they are inevitable. Thus the relevant church is an unabashed advocate of change, not only in its strategies and programs but also in its fundamental nature. For that same reason, it is also the unabashed enemy of the community. The Christian community that changes its core elements in order to make itself relevant to the perceived needs of the modern consumer will not long be a Christian community. Modern shoppers are far too capricious.

QUESTION: IS EFFICIENCY THE PROPER OBJECTIVE?

When change does occur in the modern church, we all too often allow efficiency to dictate its direction. In so doing we use a value that is, at times, contrary to both the ultimate objectives of the church and the needs of the Christian community. Nevertheless, we are tempted to let efficiency become the overriding concern of the church organization because it is perceived in our society as an absolute good.

Like the value of relevance, the desire for efficiency is not easy to tame. This is because efficiency is a perfectly proper basis on which to make some judgments. One certainly wants the church plumbing to be installed as efficiently as possible and, once specific church programs are established, one hopes that those in charge will execute them with some degree of efficiency. No sane person wishes to have his time or resources wasted. The problem comes, however, in discerning those specific instances where the use of efficiency is warranted or, more accurately, in limiting its application to such situations.

Efficiency becomes highly problematic, for example, when it begins to encroach upon and, in some cases, supplant legitimate church goals. This occurs in at least two different ways. The most obvious manifestation of this encroachment may be seen in those situations where we allow efficiency to become the central objective of any particular church program. This usually happens at the planning stage of a proposed course of action.

A committee may be established, for example, to deal with neighborhood evangelism. The ostensive purpose of such a committee, of course, is to design an efficient evangelism program that will "produce" a maximum number of converts at minimum cost. Indeed, if this were not the purpose, the committee would not have been established in the first place. We do not set up church committees to tell us *that* evangelism ought to be done, but *how* it should be administered. As a result, we move very quickly from the idea of evangelism (the manifest goal) to decisions about the means of evangelism. It is technique that absorbs all our thinking and praying, and so it is efficiency that very quickly becomes the real objective of the program.

Such an orientation leads not only to some rather counterproductive and absurd forms of evangelism (epitomized by the "gospel blimp") but also tends to spawn a church organization designed around the concept of efficiency. What it does not produce is a Christian community possessing the simple desire to share the Good News. Yes, people may be converted. Yes, people may become involved in evangelism. But in the process, the church undermines its communal base and sells its organizational future to the demon of efficiency. To what kind of community, we must ask, does the new convert come? All too often it is not one that can fulfill the promises of the evangelical salesman.

The second point at which efficiency takes its toll is at the time a program is executed. For not only do we plan programs around the objective of efficiency, but we carry them out in like manner. This is, by far, the most difficult form of efficiency to control. The reason is that efficiency is a more legitimate "guide" to the execution of a program than to its planning. Thus it has a proper role to play. Nevertheless, it can also lead to some incredible perversions.

Going back to the example of evangelism, a program designed to cultivate as many conversions as possible will inevitably include some number goals (e.g., five contacts per week). These immediate number goals can easily be translated into primary goals for those individuals who are out in the field putting the program into practice. Practitioner evangelists know that their peers will evaluate their success both by the number of contacts made and by the number of actual converts. High numbers mean peer approval. As a result, the person who actually engages in evangelism is motivated, not to build relationships with new converts, but to move on to virgin territory. The "prize" is the conversion, not the convert. It does not take much of an imagination to see what the consequences of such efficiency-motivated behavior will be, both for the convert and for the evangelist. It is clearly not an approach to human relationships commensurate with the needs of a Christian community.

It would be a mistake, however, to think that the value of efficiency is a threat merely in the area of evangelism. The menace occurs at any point where efficiency is allowed to become the ultimate objective of a church or church program. The threat, moreover, is aimed more at the community itself than at the particular program to which it may be applied. Indeed, it sometimes happens that the value of efficiency produces singularly "successful" programs (i.e., converts, funds, buildings, etc.). What it cannot produce, however, is long-term relationships or a renewed appreciation and understanding of tradition or a proper vision of what it means to be part of the family of God. Quite the contrary. It makes such exigencies a near impossibility. Those concerned with the development of the faithful community, therefore, will have to beware of the infection of efficiency.

One other point. It would be relatively easy to deal

with the problems of relevance and efficiency if they were palpably evil. That is, if both of these modern inclinations were completely pernicious (in motive or outcome), we could simply dispense with them altogether—declare them to be vermin and get rid of the little beasts once and for all. But, as we have seen, there are times when the Christian community ought to be both efficient and relevant (or, at least, related). The problem with both of these values, however, is that they are fully embraced by the spirit of modernity. Thus they come to us as imperative. Our survival often seems to depend on them. But it is this feeling of necessity that must be resisted more than the values themselves. Kept in their proper place—the background—efficiency and relevance can be helpful friends to those who work within a Christian community. But they will remain in the background only if we are fully alert to their power and seduction. Keeping them in their place today will require an attitude of resistance and a predisposition to ask nasty questions.

Resisting the urge toward efficiency and relevance, although difficult in practice, is easy to effect with the tongue. We can nod our heads, point our fingers, and exhort one another to be alert to these pitfalls of modernity. It may accomplish little, but at least we can make something of an effort. The next two questions, however, are less abstract and therefore more precarious. They are, as the saying goes, where the rubber meets the road.

QUESTION: MUST WE GROW?

Must we grow? I struggled for some time with the form of this question. The query might be more appropriately cast, "Should we want to grow?" since the real question here is one of objectives. But the problem with such a question is that it leads to a once-

and-for-all-time answer, as if the issue is one that can be resolved rather perfunctorily, never to be raised again. That is not the case, however, and so we must put the question into a form that will allow for its being asked persistently. Especially in the modern context, we must continually debate the value of growth.

What do we mean by "growth"? That is an important question since it has different meanings, depending on the context. At issue here, first of all, is *numerical* growth—not growth in wisdom, understanding, or spiritual depth. About the value of maturity, I believe, there can be no debate. It is always desirable in the Christian community and much needed in the modern world. Second, the discussion here is not about growth in the larger body of Christ, but numerical increases in the *local church*. Growth within Christ's church is a patently good thing It is something we ought to pray for on a daily basis. For a variety of reasons, however, local church growth must not be automatically linked with growth in the body of Christ. And it is the former that now beckons our attention.

Possibly the first question that ought to be asked is, Why do local churches want to grow? What is it about growth that makes it such a compelling objective? One possible answer, of course, is that growth is in and of itself a good thing. Christians who believe this tend to say, "A growing church is an exciting place to be," or, "A growing church offers increased opportunities to its members," or, "A church either grows or dies, and we want to grow so we can have a viable church organization." The problem with these responses is that they are neither obviously true nor especially biblical.

Is a growing church an exciting place to be? For many, it may be; but for others (such as the original members of a particular church), it may be the saddest

of all possible occurrences. A great many people recall
with a profound sense of loss the "original church
community." The point is not that their perspective is
necessarily correct, but that excitement is in the eye
of the beholder.

Does a growing church offer more opportunities?
Certainly. But it also eliminates the possibility of a
great many others (particularly relational opportunities).
Who is to say which are the most important?

Must a church grow in order to be viable? Clearly
the answer is no. In fact, burgeoning growth is sometimes a precursor to the death of a church, while a
steady membership can lead to organizational stability.
It all depends on what one means by "viable." The
obvious point is that growth, in and of itself, cannot
be shown to be a good thing. Indeed, from the perspective of those concerned with the development of
community, it is sometimes quite problematic.

Nor is it possible to demonstrate that the growth of
the local church is a biblical imperative. We are im-
plored to love God and our neighbor, spread the gospel, and live lives that glorify the Father, but we are
not told, "Seek first the growth of the local body."
Nor are we told that the church should *not* grow, or
that stability is good, or that declension is the proper
model. We are simply not given any specific guidelines on this issue from Scripture.

But if growth in the local church is neither an absolute good nor a biblical imperative, is it possible that
it is the logical outgrowth of being an effective Christian community? In other words, is it the consequence
of obedience to God's Word? If so, then should we
not be pleased with church growth, and is it not a
valid objective?

Once again, the problem here is that no absolute
link exists between "true Christianity" and church
growth. It may be that loving one's neighbor or shar-

ing the Good News will result in the growth of our particular church (or congregation). If so, we ought to rejoice—not in the growth of our church—but in the growth of Christ's church and the obedience of his people. But we must remember that obedience to God may lead to very different consequences. It may result in the growth of another parish, for example. Or, it may not result in church growth at all. The Bible requires us to say some very unpopular things, especially in the modern world. Confronting modernity with the biblical message on materialism or individualism, for example, will not endear us to its populace. We should not necessarily expect, therefore, that the biblical message will result in either a round of applause or the growth of our local church. Indeed, one might argue that a popular church in the modern world is, by virtue of that fact, suspect.

But that argument would neither be fair nor helpful in our quest to understand the value of growth. For the conclusion we ought to draw is that growth, on its own, is an uninterpretable statistic and somewhat meaningless. It tells us nothing, for example, about the viability, effectiveness, or genuineness of the Christian community. It may be an indication of evil (as in Jonestown) as well as good (as in Acts 2:37-42). It should bring us neither great joy nor sadness, neither pride nor humiliation. The fact of growth, in and of itself, ought to leave us unmoved.

And yet, for most of us occupying leadership positions in the local church, growth is neither meaningless nor unmoving. It is, instead, intoxicating. It makes us feel good about our church and leads almost inevitably to the conclusion that "we must be doing something right." It is fun! The question we ought to ask ourselves is, Why is that so? Why is it that even though growth is neither biblically prescribed, nor inherently good, nor necessarily an indication of true

Christianity, we receive such a charge out of it? The answer, I'm afraid, is clear. Though growth says nothing about the veracity of our witness, it says everything about the effectiveness of our organization within a competitive church market. We feel good because we are proud; we are proud because our organization is succeeding; we think we are succeeding because growth is a fundamental indicator of success in a market.

Is that necessarily wrong? What could be wrong about a little competition within the religious market? In the end, won't that simply enable us to produce a qualitatively better product? Won't the church be better off because of it?

The principal problem with modern competition is that it is essentially a contestation between Christians. The only spiritual competition sanctioned in Scripture is that which exists between the domains of good and evil; and that is not *competition*, is a *battle*. Christians, on the other hand, are to be known for their unity and love for one another. The Bible tells us nothing about competing for converts or church growth. We work together—period. That is it. Unfortunately, in the West, church growth results primarily from Christians shopping around for a "better" church. Churches do not, therefore, compete with the devil. They struggle against other Christians. And, one suspects, the Enemy is not displeased.

Competition and the concern for growth is also a major impediment to the development of genuine community. For one thing, it makes the values of relevance and efficiency nearly impossible to resist. For another, when growth becomes an objective, so do the means to growth. As a result, church functions and activities become evaluated in terms of their ability to produce growth, including such things as relationships, traditions, and vision. The ingredients of community,

however, were not designed or ever intended to produce growth. Consequently, in the modern church,
they quickly come to be seen as impediments to the
"real" mission of the church. In such circumstances,
they cannot survive. Nor can the faithful community.

So where does this leave us? It seems that we are
left with the need, first of all, to be rid of the idea
that growth is valuable. Growth simply should not be
a basis of consideration in the decision-making proc-
esses of the local church. This does not mean that
growth should be ignored if it happens. Certainly, a
church must make decisions in terms of the size of its
congregation, and this will include the need to account for increases and decreases in size. But growth
per se should not be the objective. If growth happens
in the process of our being a Christian community
(and it may), then we should rejoice in the *being*, not
in the *growth*. Organizationally, the growing church
will have to deal with growth as a matter of concern,
since it will lead both to some new opportunities and
to a number of significant problems. Indeed, it is
much more difficult to function as a community when
a church becomes large (and thus some congregations
may want to split in order to preserve the benefits of
a small community). But the crucial thing is not to
desire church growth. It is a passion unworthy of the
Christian community.

Bridling the spirit of seeking growth for growth's
sake in the modern church will not be easy. We are
too thoroughly drenched with the assumption of the
value of growth—in everything from business (where
it might be a proper goal) to zucchini squash (where
there ought to be limits!)—to check its march with
hope alone. On the other hand, to stubbornly resist
growth at every turn is not only to blunder into an
equally problematic error, it is also to impute to
growth an overly ominous quality. Like those who

desire growth, those who despise it are giving it a value it simply does not deserve.

What we must do, instead, is resist to the hilt any attempt to make growth a significant issue. At times, this may involve telling the advocates of "smallness" to remember the primary goals of the church. But in the modern era, it will more than likely require us to ask the cheerleaders of growth, "Must we grow? Really, *must* we grow?"

QUESTION: MUST WE MOVE?

Finally, we ought to question the impact of mobility on the faithful community. The problems of relevance, efficiency, and growth draw their social strength from mobility. It is mobility that enables (and sometimes forces) us to be religious consumers, and it is our consumptive habits that generate competition and the values of growth, efficiency, and relevance. To tackle the first three questions presented in this chapter, therefore, without raising the issue of mobility, would be foolish. The social environment that coddles these values must be questioned as thoroughly as the values themselves.

The issue of mobility needs to be addressed at two levels. The first, and most obvious, concerns the matter of intercommunity mobility. We moderns move from town to town for a variety of reasons, from finding a new job (or getting a promotion) to desiring a "better" neighborhood. Rarely considered, however, is the matter of the religious community. To be blunt, few of us would reckon the impact of our move on the religious community as an important factor in our decision-making process. We do not refuse to move from Buttonwillow to Los Angeles, for example, in order to be faithful to our religious community in Buttonwillow. Indeed, using the language of "faithfulness" in regard to such a decision seems somewhat odd to

188

us. "The Buttonwillow church does not own us! We have no moral obligation to remain a part of it. If 'the Lord is leading us' to a new position in L.A. (which just happens to involve a higher salary), we have no business denying his will just because the local church needs us. That would be absurd."

Maybe. But it would seem less so if we thought of our relationship with the local church as one involving a genuine community. For then we would be confronted with two profound truths. First, we need the religious community, and, second, it needs us as well. Or, in other words, we are a part of the church just as it is a part of us. "If one part suffers, every part suffers with it; if one part is honored, every part rejoices with it" (1 Corinthians 12:26). And if one person leaves, we all experience loss, including the one who chose to depart.

None of this implies that we should be tied irrevocably to our church community. There are times when we ought to move, and the genuine community will be able (with regret) to adjust to those occasions. But such times should be the exception, not the rule. And, most assuredly, they should involve extensive prayer and consideration of the needs of the religious community. Something else ought to be involved as well—deep pain. Anyone who can leave a church with no sense of regret or loss has never known Christian community.

More problematic than intercommunity mobility, is a second form of the phenomenon: intracommunity mobility. It is one thing to change one's place of residence (and thus one's church) as the occasion demands. It is quite another, however, to remain comfortably living in one's home while moving from church to church. Although the former represents a significant challenge for the religious community, the latter is absolutely devastating.

Why? Because the purveyors of intracommunity mobility represent the religious consumer par excellence. They are the ones who are on an eternal quest for the "best" church. Such individuals are perpetually on the lookout for a better preacher, a more advantageous social scene, or whatever. Although their stay may be brief, their influence on the church is substantial. If their wishes are not satisfied, they will take their attendance and their pocketbooks elsewhere. These are the individuals who generally represent the "gains" in the growing church as well as the "losses" in the declining congregation. They are the inspiration for our efficiency efforts and the motive behind our desire for relevance. They are probably the most insidious threat to the faithful community. And yet . . . .

And yet, I am undoubtedly one of them. At least, I am often tempted to join their ranks. Not that I have been a part of disappointing churches; I have not. Nor do I wish to suggest that I am less tempted by the wiles of relevance, or efficiency, or growth; they have their hooks in me as well. But church mobility has a special lure that I find particularly difficult to resist. Its name, I have come to believe, is self-gratification.

The problem is, I want to enjoy my Sunday-morning-worship experience. I crave to be thrilled by the music and moved by the message. I want to depart from the sanctuary feeling "uplifted and renewed," ready to face the onslaught of the week ahead. What I clearly do not want is to be bored. Or irked. Or aesthetically nauseated. When those things happen, my first thought is, *Why? Why am I sitting here subjecting myself to this ordeal? This isn't a worship service, it's a parade of pain. A masochist's delight. Why put myself through this when there is, quite possibly, an alternative just down the road* [which, in the modern world, means anything within forty miles]? *Surely God wants me to have a quality worship experience.*

Why should I put up with such mediocrity, such nonsense? It is an argument difficult to resist.

I recall an incident a number of years ago that brought this dilemma into clear relief. We were visiting some close friends in the Midwest, and, since it was Sunday, we dutifully attended Sunday morning service with them. The first thing that happened, after the standard get-them-quiet hymn, was the introduction of guests—not a general welcome, mind you, but a specific introduction of each guest by the hosts. This is standard fare in many churches, I know, but it nevertheless gives me the heebiejeebies. Well, our friend, being a rather articulate and erudite fellow, pulled us through that uneasy situation with his usual aplomb, but I could sense that this was not going to be one of our more meaningful worship experiences.

And it was not. The music was less than superb, the announcements were legion, and the sermon was not to be believed—literally. The high point of the message occurred when the pastor, pounding on the pulpit, reminded us of the importance of the "Masonic law." Dumbfounded at first, I eventually realized that he meant the "Mosaic law," not the rules of the Masons. After that, my mind closed completely (though my sense of humor kept right on working briskly). I heard no more of the sermon.

When we left the church, I could not but wonder how our dear wise friends (he, a professor of philosophy; she, his intellectual equal) could tolerate such an assembly. And, not only did they tolerate it, but they were fully involved—as deacon, teachers, committee members, etc. When I was able to put that question before them (in my own gallant manner: "How can you endure such imbecility?!"), they responded apologetically that there were no "good reasons" for their attendance. They explained that, originally, they went because it was the nearest church of their denomination. Once they became members, however, they continued their involvement, despite a growing realization that the church was beset with a host of problems, because they felt a sense of responsibility to that community. That was it. Obligation and duty. They could come up with nothing more substantial.

At the time, their reasons for involvement were incomprehensible to me. These reasons seemed to run counter to the laws of nature and the rules of right living. And, of course, I was correct in this assessment. The natural law they abridged was the one concerning self-gratification; the rule they obviated was the principle of self-protection. What these standards ignore, and what our friends found compelling, was the need to be faithful to a Christian community. What they knew then, and what I realized much later, is that such a community cannot survive if its members live by the fickle standards of self-gratification.

The undeniable truth is that if we wish to build a genuine Christian community, we must resist the urge to continually shop around for the perfect worship service. Certainly we should not put up with heresies in belief or practice. Nothing, including the need for community, can justify that. But once we are part of a church that is theologically correct, we must commit ourselves to the people of that congregation. This will not be easy. Periodically it will mean putting up with Sunday morning services that are not altogether uplifting or delightful or entertaining. But nothing militates against community like the desire to be entertained. Ultimately the Christian community will come into existence only when modern Christians replace the desire to feel good on Sunday with the passion to participate fully in the body of Christ.

For the church itself, however, it means very little—at least, by way of direct action. Even though the church community is the big loser in the game of church switching, it is nevertheless in a very poor position to do much about its plight. Some might argue that the church can guard against the influence of church switchers by paying attention only to those in the congregation who are long-standing members. But this is surely a poor policy from a Christian perspective, since new members should not be considered irrelevant or inferior simply because they are new, nor does the Christian community have the right to ignore them. Indeed, it must incorporate them fully and immediately. Others might suggest that the local church should teach and implore its parishioners to be faithful members of the community, reminding them regularly of their responsibilities to the local church. However, though the church ought to encourage relationships, uphold traditions, and sustain its vision, it is not in the business of (shall we say) blowing its own horn, nor should it attempt to hold its members by threat of fire and brimstone or the wrath of God (or preacher).

We must accept the fact that the church's role in dealing with the problem of switching is not primarily one of exhortation but of function. The best thing it can do is to *be* the kind of Christian community God intended. It is our responsibility as community members to live up to the obligations implied in that relationship. It is we—not the local church—who need to confront the mobility compulsion with the question, "Must we move?"

CONCLUSION

My Dear Wormwood,

You mentioned casually in your last letter that the patient has continued to attend one church, and one only, since he was converted, and that he is not wholly pleased with it. May I ask what you are about? Why have I no report on the causes of his fidelity to the parish church? Do you realise that unless it is due to indifference it is a very bad thing? Surely you know that if a man can't be cured of churchgoing, the next best thing is to send him all over the neighborhood looking for the church that suits him until he becomes a taster or connoisseur of churches.

The reasons are obvious. In the first place the parochial organisation should always be attacked, because, being a unity of place and not of likings, it brings people of different classes and psychology together in the kind of unity the Enemy desires. The congregational principle, on the other hand, makes each church into a kind of club, and finally, if all goes well, into a coterie or faction. In the second place, the search for a "suitable" church makes the man a critic where Enemy wants him to be a pupil. What He wants of the layman in church is an attitude which may, indeed, be critical in the sense of rejecting what is false or unhelpful, but which is wholly uncritical in the sense that it does not appraise—does not waste time in thinking about what it rejects, but lays itself open in uncommenting, humble receptivity to any nourishment that is going. (You see how grovelling, how unspiritual, how irredeemably vulgar He is!) This attitude, especially during sermons, creates the condition (most hostile to our whole policy) in which platitudes can become really audible to a human soul. There is hardly any sermon, or any book, which may not be dangerous to us if it is received in this temper. So pray bestir yourself and send this fool the round of the neighbouring churches as soon as possible. Your record up to date has not given us much satisfaction. . . .

Your affectionate uncle
SCREWTAPE

(From C. S. Lewis, *Screwtape Letters* [New York: Macmillan, 1950], pp. 81–82.)

194

thirteen / Laboring on Behalf of the Faithful Community

Finally, there is work to be done. The building of a faithful community will not be accomplished by the affirmation of Christian values alone nor by the simple questioning of the spirit of modernity. It will also require a willingness to work patiently but persistently toward the development of a Christian community. Such a goal will be neither quickly nor easily accomplished. As we have seen, many social circumstances obstruct this objective and many values mitigate against its realization. Nevertheless, by the grace of God and the obedience of his people, it surely can be done. It is my hope that the following suggestions will be helpful to those who accept this challenge. These suggestions, however, represent, not techniques for community construction (heaven forbid!), but guidelines for those who wish to invest themselves in the work of the Christian community. The value of these suggestions lies less in what they are than in what they provoke within the heart and mind of the community builder.

STOP, LOOK, AND LISTEN

It would be a tragic irony, indeed, if in our rush to build a genuine Christian community, we began dismantling those elements of community that already exist. I have seen many church traditions scuttled in the name of community development—trashed as impediments to the attainment of a "real" community. Such behavior results from the misguided notion that community development is more technique than a state of being. This is essentially a modernist approach to community life and, as such, is doomed to failure. It will inevitably be tripped up by its inherent—but latent—contracommunity values. The trash heap is no place to begin the exercise of community building.

Rather, the first task of the community builder is to take stock of the existent structure. What is already in place? What traditions are worth cherishing? Which relationships are the most durable? What vision already inspires us? These are the places to begin our efforts in community, and these are the building blocks on which a genuine community can be erected. It is true, of course, that there will be some items that may be deemed "unworthy"—a few traditions that really do not belong. But these must be discarded with great care and consideration, after they have been fully tested against the judgment of God's Word and the traditional wisdom of Christ's church. Reclamation, not dispossession, is the chief task of those engaged in community development.

To that end, let me also insert a plea for tolerance and receptivity to some of the historical traditions of the Christian faith. The last four or five hundred years of Christian history have been marked by a great deal of boundary-maintenance activity, much of it concerned with the need of one Christian community to dissociate itself from the traditions of others. Although this sort of thing may have been necessary in the sixteenth century, it seems rather unfruitful in the twentieth. Indeed, I have become increasingly convinced that in our efforts to sift out the chaff from the wheat, we have discarded numerous valuable grains of tradition from the church—traditions that have brought inspiration and understanding to millions of Christians throughout the ages.

This, I think, is a tragedy. If we are intent on throwing out every Christian tradition that has ever been tainted by misuse or misappropriation, then we are destined to worship naked and alone. Our goal should be the restoration of worthy traditions, not their destruction. And, while some Christians will find this call for tolerance difficult to embrace, I urge the reader to give it serious consideration. The genuine Christian community deserves no less.

Define the Community

Of all my suggestions, this one is without doubt the most dangerous. We moderns have a tendency to define and redefine the essence of something in perpetuity. We do this, I believe, because we are in constant need of ideological justification for structural changes that we wish to make. Conceptual rationalization has become something of an art form in the modern church.

Nevertheless, there must be times when we perform the conceptual task—times to ask who we are and what we wish to become; times to ask how the vision of the Christian church translates into specific objectives for a particular Christian community; times to ask questions about governance, and creeds, and bylaws. In some Christian communities, such defining activities will be accomplished at the congregational level, while in others it will be done by select committees within the church, conference, denomination, synod, or whatever. I am much less concerned about where it is done than about the fact that it *is* done—thoroughly, self-consciously, prayerfully, reverently, thoughtfully. And I am concerned that it be done consistently within the parameters of Holy Scripture and the historical vision of the Christian church.

The last point is an important one. Defining the community is neither an excuse to begin something new nor a means to realize the dreams of a charismatic personality. Such times of definition take place within the context of authority, not outside of it. They are attempts, not to determine what the authority is, but to come to an understanding of the implications of established authority for the life of a particular religious community.

If such is not the case, then the effort to define the community will doom its ostensive purpose. To begin the defining process with the needs of a specific group (regardless of how genuine) or the aspirations of a particular individual (regardless of how sage) is the surest route to folly. It is based on the modern assumption that we are the source of our own inspiration, the final arbiters of our own existence. But the Christian community is fundamentally opposed to such thinking. It defines itself, not for the purpose of creativity, but in order to understand what it is supposed to be. Affirmation, not invention, is its primary goal.

Get On With It

If community definition is the most dangerous suggestion I have made, then "Get on with it" may be the most important. Despite its vernacular form, it is not an easy thing to do in the modern context. For the spirit of change requires relevance. And that means we must constantly be checking the wind with an outstretched wet finger, adjusting course, and reshaping the purpose of the journey. Such mid-course corrections are not only time consuming, they also divert attention from the task at hand. And the primary task of the Christian community is not defining its purposes and objectives, but pursuing them.

Getting on with it, then, simply means that once we know what we are (definition), we ought to cease the debate over purpose and begin the task of functioning as a Christian community. This in no way implies that we should forget about ends or concentrate on means. The goal here is not to ignore ends, but to stop arguing over them—to accept them as givens and pursue instead the implications of the assumptions that we hold. The one thing that inevitably destroys Christian community is the constant need to reassess the fundamentals. It leads to the feeling that everything is up for grabs—that at any particular church meeting or congregational assembly, anything can happen. It also leads to interminable periods of navel gazing and self-assessment. What it clearly does not produce is an operational community.

Limiting debate on the essentials—in the modern era—will be an almost impossible task. People are convinced of their right to question anything and everything that comes along. Thus if someone's pet concern is being (or is perceived to be) sidestepped by the church, that person will feel no compunction at all about blaming the "problem" on the assumptions

199

of the community. Such people, in my opinion, must be lovingly but firmly reminded that, while they certainly have the right to their own opinions, their concerns will be evaluated from the perspective of the community's vision, and not vice versa. They must be made aware of the fact that it is not the definition of the community that is up for debate but the propriety of the complaint.

Those who bring such complaints to the church, of course, will be nonplused by this kind of response. The community will be branded with such labels as "elitist," "dogmatic," and "irrelevant." But such hyperbole clearly misses the point. The Christian community is, by definition, elitist in the sense that its vision does not result from plebiscite; it is dogmatic in the sense that it affirms certain truths; and it is irrelevant in the sense that it refuses to accommodate its vision to the whims of modernity. None of this means, however, that the Christian community is any less loving or compassionate (it is also a common fiction that love and dogma are mutually exclusive). Quite the reverse. It is the community that, confident of its vision, will possess the time and energy necessary to practice the love of Christ. Bickering over the community's identity never loved a soul.

Give Community Traditions the Benefit of the Doubt

I have already made a plea for tolerance in relation to the historical traditions of the church and have argued (ad nauseam) concerning their necessity and importance. It will be no surprise to the reader, therefore, that I believe Christian traditions ought to be given the benefit of the doubt within the religious community. Once in place, traditions within a particular church should not be the object of continual review and assessment. Such a procedure rather rapidly erodes the community's confidence in the tradition as well as its value to the community as a whole.

This erosion occurs, not because the tradition cannot stand up to rational scrutiny, but because constant reassessment diverts attention from the thing being symbolized (e.g., the crucifixion) to the symbol itself (e.g., the crucifix). Since the material object or ritual is not itself the point of the tradition, such diversions (over a period of time) render the tradition meaningless. Under these circumstances it will not be long before it is sloughed off as useless (see chapters 3–4). And this is an unmitigated tragedy to those who would covet the faithful community.

To avoid such tragedies requires more than simply hoping no one will question the value of a tradition, however. It necessitates, rather, a high degree of vigilance over the use of traditions within the community. One of the most devastating blows a tradition can suffer is to be used hypocritically as an excuse for injustice. People, both within and outside the religious community, are not blind. They will discover such hypocrisy readily and draw their own inferences. Unfortunately, one of the conclusions often reached is that the tradition so used is a worthless sham, a religious veneer that covers the actor's real intentions and motives. Thus the tradition is often pronounced guilty along with the hypocrite. Although this conclusion is not necessarily logical nor warranted, it is nevertheless common. Nothing, and no one, so thoroughly undermines tradition as the hypocrite. It is the falsely pious who bring down religious traditions—not the ungodly.

But how does the religious community guard against the dastardly effects of hypocrisy? The answer is easily given but difficult to put into practice: it must be done by personal confrontation. Hypocrites must be approached by other members of the community and made aware of their own pretense. Such an approach not only has the greatest chance of bringing about a change in behavior, but it also attacks the cause of the problem (the hypocrite) and not the symptom (misuse of tradition).

Unfortunately, confrontation seems to be the least used strategy in the modern church. The reason is not difficult to discern. Confrontation requires a level of community esprit de corps rarely found in the twentieth-century church. We have neither the community concern nor the backbone to engage in such quiet diplomacy. Thus we do the typically modern thing— we set up a committee to study it. And what is the result of a committee investigation? Not a personal struggle with hypocrisy. Not a Nathan, looking deception straight in the face and saying, "Thou art the man." No, the committee comes up with a recommendation for some structural change that it believes will "avoid the problem in the future." This means, in all likelihood, that the committee will support a change in the tradition itself in order to prevent its misuse in the future. In other words, to ameliorate the pain of personal confrontation, we cast the blame on the tradition rather than on the sinner. Only we moderns would be capable of throwing away the treasures of antiquity to avoid a moment of interpersonal discomfort.

That is a tragedy. It is a tragedy because, as we have seen, traditions are invaluable to the faithful community. Instead of putting them in the dock, we ought to put them at center stage, giving them the honor that is their due. More than that, we should enjoy them. For some reason, we have come not only to mistrust traditions but also to bear them as a kind of historical burden—as a heavy load that we must endure in order to placate the past. But traditions are not an encumbrance to be tolerated; they are a blessing to be celebrated. We ought to enter into them

with great joy and jubilation, relishing the memories
they evoke and delighting in the God of whom they
remind us. More than giving traditions the benefit of
the doubt, we should give them the benefit of our
gratitude and respect. Surely, such reminders of our
heritage deserve no less.

Be Patient With Sharp Corners and Rough Edges

One of the casualties of the "successful" church is
the oddball—the person who does not quite fit into
the societal ideal with regard to appearance, personality, intelligence, etc. When success is defined in terms
of consumer appeal, people who are not considered
attractive are an impediment to the church's success.

The modern church attempts to cultivate a certain
image in order to win the allegiance of the consumer.
No one wants to be identified with a community of
peculiar people! We want, rather, to see ourselves
among others who are (at least) at our level of status
and social savoir-faire. This means, minimally, that the
successful church must choose leaders who meet the
modern criteria for attractiveness. More than likely, it
also means that its members are a bit embarrassed by
those in their midst who are strange, idiomatic, funky,
or worse.

The desire to congregate with "fine folk" is certainly not a modern impulse. It is a human appetite of
long-standing reputation. But in the days of Peter
Peasant the place of worship was more a matter of
geography than anything else. One may have been
careful to sit in pews with one's social peers, but the
church itself was made up of a wide range of social
types. In the modern church, however, we see a much
more stratified group of worshipers—people of stand-
ardized class, race, status, and lifestyle. Such homogeneity, of course, results from the feasibility of choice.
With the modern possibility of selecting the church of

one's fancy, the old human desire for conformity has been transformed into the "right" to worship with clones and look-alikes.

The faithful community, I believe, must actively seek to resist this process of homogeneity, not by artificially trying to force heterogeneous peoples to worship together, but by expanding tolerance for those who are different. One response that I think ought to be avoided is creating a special kind of program to force a variegated populace on the church. For a host of sociological and psychological reasons, I think this is a poor approach to the problem. It rarely works, for one thing, and it often destroys the community it is attempting to cultivate. The need, rather, is for a conscious tolerance of those who are defined as "different" within the church. It may mean reaching out to those who have personality quirks. It may involve a deliberate effort to interact with those who are of another class or ethnic background. It may mean subjecting oneself to people who are fundamentally irritating and even obnoxious. More than anything, however, it means blinding oneself to the social appraisals of people within the religious community.

The fundamental question for the Christian community is not what the prestige of a member can do for us but what the church can accomplish in the lives of its people. That question may not lead to "success" within the modern context but it will produce a modicum of tolerance within the church toward those whom the world labels peculiar. Its harvest, in other words, will be the faithful community.

BE SLOW TO BUREAUCRATIZE

To allay suspicions that I am some sort of anti-bureaucratic madman, and also to set the context for the following recommendations, let me state that "a bureaucracy is not an inherently evil organizational structure." I have worked in a variety of bureaucratic settings, both within and outside of the church, and have engaged in a modest degree of study relative to bureaucratic function. Both my experience and study indicate that, at times, bureaucratic organization is the best (or only) means of meeting certain worthy objectives.

Nevertheless, as was discussed earlier, there are also some significant problems with bureaucracy, notably for those within the religious community. Bureaucracies are designed to regularize human behavior—to make it efficient, follow certain codified standards, and meet particular objectives. Those who believe that bureaucracy is *the* answer to the ills of the church assume that organizational behavior must be planned, predicted, and controlled; hence, they are inherently suspicious of spontaneous activity, especially by those at the lower end of the organizational chart.

As a church bureaucratizes, therefore, it becomes increasingly dominated by organizational concerns (survival, efficiency, planning, control, rules) and decreasingly absorbed with the basic elements of community, especially relationships and traditions. Although the bureaucratized church may be in a good position to do a few things quite effectively, it is in a rather poor position to be, in practice, a genuine community. With genuineness at stake, those who care about the life of the Christian community must be wary of the need to bureaucratize.

The dilemma before the modern church, then, is this: If bureaucratic organization is helpful in some circumstances, but potentially threatening to the life of the community, how shall the church respond? It would be so much easier if bureaucracy were patently evil or inherently virtuous. At least we could then either banish or embrace it and forget about the consequences. Unfortunately, the real world does not allow us to operate so indiscriminately. Wisdom, in this case (as in most cases), requires thoughtful consideration, not simplistic response. To help the community move in that direction, therefore, let me suggest three questions—questions that ought to be asked by the faithful community prior to the implementation of any particular bureaucratic arrangement:

1. *"Is there really a need?"* The desire to bureaucratize is quite often a good one. Someone with an organizing bent sees a need (e.g., people in need of clothing, comfort, a social life, etc.) and proceeds to establish an organization to meet the perceived need. Unfortunately, perceiving a need is sometimes a rather subjective procedure. What I may see as a need might actually be a product of my imagination or the pet interest of someone else in the church.

People are capable of verbally expressing all kinds of needs, and such verbal expressions may or may not correlate with reality. Quite often those who point out "needs" in the church are themselves in need—they need recognition, or company, or relationships, or they simply need to be needed. This is not to suggest that we should ignore such expressions of need; they should be taken seriously. But we should not take them at face value, nor should we build a bureaucratic structure to meet them before we are convinced the needs are absolutely genuine.

2. *"Does the need require an organizational response?"* Let us assume that the answer to the first question is yes, and we are convinced that, indeed, there is a genuine need. The question now becomes: How do we meet the need? This is a crucial question, the answer to which must not be automatically assumed.

The facile response, when once a need is recognized, is to set up an organization to study the problem and develop a plan to meet it. Such a response is easy, both because it placates the demands of those who are most agitated about the need and because it relieves the rest of us from worrying about it for any length of time. In fact, this is why a committee is sometimes set up to deal with purely fictitious needs—it gets the rabble-rousers off everyone's back for a few months (or even years!). But even if the need is genuine, the organizational response is not necessarily the best one. Not only does it put the community further down the road toward bureaucratization, but it assumes that a committee (or team of specialists) is best equipped to deal with the need. This is a very modern assumption, but quite often wrong, especially in a religious community.

Whether the need is to share the gospel or share the wealth, a great variety of options are available to the church—options that do not necessitate a bureaucratic structure. One response, which I highly recommend, is prayer. It involves simply the presentation of the need before the community as a whole and an extended time of corporate and private prayer. When supplication has been made, the community leaves the action in the hands of God and his Spirit working in the lives of his people. There is nothing magical in this approach nor is it necessarily antiorganizational in nature (since the Spirit moves organizations as well as individuals). It simply assumes that God's people, acting in good faith and prayer, will accomplish the tasks God puts before them. Instead of a committee being responsible, everyone assumes responsibility; instead of faith being placed in an organizational structure, it is placed in God and the church body that Christ has established. Although in some cases this may eventually result in an organizational structure to handle the problem, it will more than likely produce a variety of creative efforts to meet the need. The latter possibility is an exciting one, both for those who have never experienced it before and for those who are wary of bureaucracy.

3. *"Should the organizational response be temporary?"* Even if a perceived need is genuine and is determined to require an organizational response, the Christian community should consider the possibility of setting up an impermanent structure to deal with the problem. This is desirable, in my opinion, because it guards against the bureaucratic tendency toward survival and growth.

All of us have seen or been a part of church committees that exist in perpetuity despite the lack of any evidence whatsoever that they are needed or useful. This occurs when committee members come to believe that their purpose is to *function* rather than to *serve,* and church leaders do not have the heart to tell them otherwise. Unfortunately, the perceived needs of one year are not the perceived needs of another. If committees are allowed to continue to exist, regardless of need, churches will soon find themselves living with more committees than members and with a totally uncontrollable bureaucracy.

The only solution to committee proliferation is the "perishable committee"—one designed explicitly to terminate at some point in the future. In my opinion, aside from a few standing committees, every committee within the Christian community ought to be perishable. It should have to prove its worth in order to survive—not to the committee members (who will rarely, if ever, admit to their organization's uselessness), but to the community as a whole. Unneeded committees are not only a treacherous waste of time and energy, they are also a significant threat to the life of the faithful community. That is a thought worth pondering every time a well-meaning parishioner stands up and says, "I see a need that we ought to address and I think we should—"

One parenthetical point. Nothing that has been stated, implied, or otherwise communicated about the quagmire of bureaucracy should be interpreted to suggest that order is a problem for the Christian community. Order is not only a substantially different phenomenon from bureaucracy, but it is also an essential ingredient of community worship, administration, and general function. No community can last long without it. The fact that order is sometimes confused with bureaucracy is one of modernity's more regrettable—though understandable—aberrations. It stems both from bureaucracy's orderly requirements and the tendency of its advocates to justify bureaucratic recommendations on the basis of the need for order. But, although bureaucracy requires order, order does not need bureaucracy (and, in most cases, is much healthier without it). Order is a disposition without which we could not even communicate; bureaucracy is a structure of authority without which we could no doubt communicate with far more ease and lucidity.

PONDERING THE ROLE OF THE CLERGY

If we are to move the modern church toward community, we must very carefully reconsider the role of the clergy. At the very least, the image of the pastor as a supersalesman must be radically attenuated, not only for the sake of the community but also for the benefit of the pastor's psyche. As long as the Sunday-morning service is considered the foremost event and singular function of the church, we will not have community. To consider it such, forces all the members, including the pastor, to invest most of their energy into getting ready for that "event," and it fosters a showman's mindset for all who have leadership roles in the service. It encourages those in the pews to assume the disposition of an audience; they become merely onlookers seeking to be entertained. Most of all, it nourishes the assumption that the layman is a religious consumer who sits back and peruses what the church has to offer in the way of amusement and diversion. If a listener likes what the pastor has to say, he or she might stick around for a little while. Otherwise, it's on to the next show.

It is sometimes argued today that the "television preacher" is stealing the audience from the local church and that no church can possibly compete with the glitter, gold, and tinsel of the electronic church service. For this dilemma, the television preacher is often blamed. It seems to me, however, that the problem here may be less with the television service than with the services at the local church, or, more accurately, with the modern image of what a church service should involve. If the local church functioned as a Christian community—if the layman felt like a participant at the morning service rather than a spectator at a sideshow—then the electronic church simply would not be able to compete. It is precisely because we have made our church services showlike that the televised church service has been able to succeed. They simply do a better job of it; they have the facilities to put on a better show. They have adapted more effectively to the demands of the modern religious market.

If we are to escape the religious-market syndrome (and I think the life of the Christian community depends on our doing so), we must modify the contemporary model of the Sunday morning church service—and this means having a different image of the pastor's role. With regard to the service, we must somehow take the onus off the pastor to "produce a great show" and place it on the members to participate in a genuine worship service. The goal, in my opinion, should not be just to hear an inspiring message from the pastor, but to participate in the worship of God. Does this mean that the sermon ought to be eliminated? Certainly not. Biblical teaching is an important ingredient in a genuine worship service. But the sermon is only one means of teaching and only one aspect of the service. It is not the whole ball of wax!

But if the sermon were a smaller portion of the service, would that not shift the emphasis away from "the Word"? Not necessarily. In fact, it ought to enhance it. We who label ourselves evangelical Christians have come to believe that the sermon should be the focus of the morning service because it assures the centrality of the Word. Unfortunately, it assures only the centrality of the preacher. Indeed, anyone who fully identifies a sermon with "the Word" is two steps down the path to heresy. Such thinking has led many pastors to become cult leaders and not a few parishioners to profound grief. The sermon is many things (it can be instruction, encouragement, rebuke, solace, etc.), but it is not the Word. It is, rather, the word of a human being, presumably inspired by God's Spirit and guided by his instruction, but it is not the Word of God. To think otherwise is perilous for the Christian and a substantial threat to the Christian community.

If the service is not a show, then what is it? One thing it should not be is sloppy or half-baked or disorderly. Nor is it to be entered into casually or without due reverence and preparation. Since the service is not a show, it follows logically that we are not the audience: God is. The service is for him and it ought to be carried out in a manner he would find satisfying. To me, this implies a quality service, filled with awe, beauty, praise, and order. Such a service is punctuated by a recognition and use of many of the good gifts in God's creation and participated in by all the people in the congregation. The community comes together, as one in Christ, to worship their Creator. They do not come to be inspired by the pastor but to be inspired by the wonders of the One they worship. Whatever happens in worship should involve *all* who attend, directing them away from the means of worship and toward the Object of their devotion.

If the pastor is not the ringleader of the show, then what is he? Well, the word *pastor* (Ephesians 4:11) means "shepherd," presenting a picture of one who tends and cares for a flock. In our world that means someone who is able to guide his flock around the dangers of modernity, not into them. He does this, like any pastor in any era, by guarding against the wolves of perversion (Acts 20:29), declaring the *whole* counsel of God (v. 27), and teaching sound doctrine (Titus 2:1). He does this also by interceding on behalf of his sheep, praying for them and others who care for them, that they may be able to carry out the tasks to which God has called them (1 Timothy 2:1–2). He does this especially by serving those in his charge as Peter counsels:

> Be shepherds of God's flock that is under your care, serving as overseers—not because you must, but because you are willing, as God wants you to be; not greedy for money, but eager to serve, not lording it over those entrusted to you, but being examples to the flock. And when the Chief Shepherd appears, you will receive the crown of glory that will never fade away (1 Peter 5:2–4).

What crown of glory does the modern pastor seek? What crown of glory do we urge him to pursue? All too often it is the modern success story, replete with adoring audiences, large sanctuaries, and even larger paychecks. If we wish to have Christian community, if we wish our pastors to enjoy the crown of glory that never fades away, then we must discard modernity's image of a successful pastor. The pastor's first responsibility is to God—not to the market. And his primary mission is to serve the flock—not to rustle sheep from another shepherd's pasture. Would that our pastors might accept such a mission. Would that we might let them do so.

CONCLUSION

The faithful community is, above all, a worshiping community. The One it worships is the God of the universe, the Lord of creation. It does not worship the pastor or the choir director or the missionary; nor does it worship any other aspect of the community, including its own traditions or communal relationships. All of these things—all of its people—work together for the glory of God. When the glory is heaped on the community or on any one of its elements, then the community ceases to be faithful. But when people gather in faithful obedience to the One who has called them and focus their devotion on him, then the Source of their togetherness is glorified and the future of their community is assured. For who shall separate them from the love of God?

PART VI / The Intimate Community

fourteen / Mutual Commitments

As we approach the task of community building within the context of the family, we need to remember what this project is about. My goal is not so much to provide handy-dandy techniques for family development as it is to suggest ways that the family community can be strengthened. How may we quicken our vision of the intimate community? How may family relationships be nurtured? How can preservative traditions be sustained? These are the kinds of questions that invite the imaginations of those who seek community in the midst of the modern family.

A Tasteless Journey

For some who read these pages, I know the above paragraph is a disappointment. After all, the one thing we have come to count on these days from treatises about the family is a little spice. "Surely you're not going to put us through three chapters of family suggestions without being suggestive?" I hear someone saying. "No love among the elect? No sex for suffering servants? Not even a Cosmo Survey to show us what we're all missing? Don't we deserve at least that much for buying the book?"

I am not a prude. Nor am I beyond purchasing a book with a modicum of titillation. I even maintain a close association with someone who subscribes to *Sports Illustrated* in order (I am convinced) to receive the benefits of its swimsuit edition! Nevertheless, I wish to write nothing that would imply that the communal problems of the modern family can be resolved with a bit of *la dolce vita*. Whatever some novel sexual technique may do for the love life of a particular couple (and, who knows, it may catapult them to the heights of ecstasy), it will do nothing to strengthen the intimate community. Indeed, it may effect substantial harm. To the extent that we believe new techniques will solve family problems, we have bought into the illusion of other possibilities—the fantasy that something new and different will finally satisfy us. But the first step toward a familial community is not to reach for something "out there," but to look deeply into the heart of the one who lives here.

The Quandary of Commitment

How much do I desire to be a part of the intimate community? That is both the starting point of one's quest and the crucial issue throughout the journey. Its saliency derives not from its personalistic character but from its social location. We live in a society that offers little social support for genuine community; in fact, much of its influence is relationally destructive. Peter Peasant may have been able to take community for granted, but we moderns cannot. As a result, we find ourselves in the very unenviable position of having to volitionally decide *for* community in a world that is decidedly against it. It is an unenviable position in part because such a decision is hard to make. It is unenviable also because it involves a contradiction in terms.

How does one obtain community from personal commitment? The thing is all wrong. Community is the context for commitment, not the result of it. It is community's vision that inspires commitment. It is community's tradition that keeps commitment from degenerating into self-interest (a characteristic of modernity). And it is community's relationships that provide the framework for commitment. So how can we begin with commitment and end up with community? How can we start with the dependent variable?

Where else can we start? All other options are either unavailable, unethical, or self-defeating. The best way to experience community, for example, is to attach oneself to an already existing community; but alas, unless one is willing to be sequestered from modernity for life, few such communities are available for adoption. One could, of course, establish a community by force, assuming one had the appropriate resources (power, wealth, and charisma). Hitler tried this in Germany, but his approach hardly seems the ideal standard for a Christian community. And then there are all those great suggestions from modernity—from Listerine to deodorized underwear—guaranteed to cement any relationship for eternity.

None of those efforts will do. As difficult as it may be to carry off and as difficult as it may be to even

219

conceptualize, we must nevertheless face the fact that in the context of modernity the intimate community will rise or fall on the issue of commitment. There is no other alternative. This means, at least in the short run, that modernity is the victor. It has forced even those who rail against it to play by its rules—to use one of its choices to create the thing undermined by choice. But if the ploy is successful, modernity—not community—will be the one forced to make the accommodation.

FEELING THE COMMITMENT

Success, however, will not be easily achieved. There is, for one thing, a problem of terminology. What I mean by "commitment" diverges substantially from the current meaning of the word. It is not uncommon, for example, to hear "commitment" applied to some level of feeling. For example, in the realm of romance, one commits oneself to a particular relationship at the point one feels a sufficient degree of "tingle." Regardless of how meaningful such a commitment may be to those involved (and one certainly hopes for the best), it is a far cry from the kind of commitment needed to sustain communal relationships.

When commitment is dependent on feelings, it will generate nothing resembling an intimate community. Feelings are volatile and fleeting, as well they should be. No one would enjoy relating to someone whose feelings were always on a level plane. Not only would such persons be a bit of an embarrassment at funerals and parties, they would also be something less than fully human. Feelings are legitimately the product of commitments—as well as of circumstances and body chemistry—but hardly the stuff of a solid commitment itself.

But can't feelings turn into commitments and thus be the precursors of community? Possibly. At its best, this seems to be the point of the modern wedding ceremony: it takes two individuals who are romantically involved and seals the relationship with a commitment. The problem, however, is that as long as the commitment finds its justification in feelings, it can be "legitimately" aborted when the feelings depart. In the case of a marriage, for example, the promise of faithfulness "till death do us part," though heartily felt at the time of the ceremony, can appear contingent in retrospect. This is especially the case if one develops those same feelings for someone else. If such feelings made the first commitment legitimate, why should they not perform the same function in the future? To what does one owe greater loyalty—the creator (feelings) or the created (commitment)? When feelings become god, it is difficult to bow before another.

THE COMMITMENT OF SUCCESS

But there are other rivals to commitment besides feelings. There is, for example, the modern idea of success. Personal success is a powerful motivator in the modern world. It is the primary reason we are urged to get an education and select an occupation (we also do this for "self-fulfillment," though there is a surprisingly high correlation between job satisfaction and compensation), church, neighborhood, and lifestyle. Relationships, too, can be chosen for success, and not a few friends and acquaintances are nurtured for precisely that purpose. Indeed, it is not unknown for such a criterion to weigh heavily in the selection of a spouse.

Material success is a powerful motivator in the modern world because it has become our standard for personal worth and identity. While Peter Peasant may have dreamed of becoming rich so that he could be *rich* (i.e., enjoy all the good things of richdom), Martin Modern dreams of becoming rich so that he can be *somebody*. Though the reasons for this shift cannot be pursued here, their impact on relationships must be addressed. When self-worth becomes linked to material success, social achievement is a matter of immense personal significance. To fail is to *be* a failure; to succeed is to *be* successful. Nothing could be more important. Nothing and no one.

As a result, relationships must play second fiddle to success. In some cases, this means that relationships are reduced to mechanisms for achievement; conduits in someone's search for significance. The modern business relationship, for example, is explicitly designed for that purpose, as is one's relationship with the teller, the grocery clerk, and the salesperson. Even the modern pastor can fall victim to such relationships, either as the one being used or the one who uses relationships for personal success.

In the family, however, the temptation is not so much to use relationships to promote personal achievement (though the spouse at the proverbial business party may feel so used) as to make them subordinate objectives. Thus the needs of family relationships must conform to the pattern set by the drive for success. The standard example of this phenomenon, of course, is the father who spends so much time at his job that he has little time for his wife and children; however, I think that is an artifact of a bygone era. Modern family relationships are not subverted by the success fantasies of the father, but by the achievement needs of *every* family member. Johnny must be the best piano player, Mary must become student government president, daddy must be the best sociologist, and mother must become chairperson of the board. Indeed, the achievement of each individual family member seems to be the primary objective of the self-fulfilling family.

The question is, How does one even begin to form

a communal commitment in a society that honors only individual success? How can the rewards of relational commitments, which are clearly intangible, stack up against the accolades of personal achievement? Is my commitment to my spouse really more important than occupational prestige? More significantly, am I honestly willing to put my relational commitments above self-gratification? Are my commitments really more important than success? Although our rhetoric is full of reassuring phrases, our actions are less convincing. And the intimate community needs our actions.

A MATTER OF RECRUITMENT

There are other impediments to communal commitment, of course, some of which are peculiar to modernity (e.g., problems of choice and other-fulfillment) and others that are not (e.g., human depravity). The need at this point, however, is not to enumerate the difficulties, but to come up with a solution. Given the problems of commitment in the modern world, is it possible to generate a viable commitment to the intimate community? The answer, I believe, is 'Yes, but—"

The "yes" part of the answer comes from the Christian vision of who we are as human beings. We have wills, and we are responsible. We were created in such a way that we can will to do some things, just as we can will not to do others. However, we neither develop nor find our expression in isolation. We are both affected by our social circumstances and, in turn, affect others. On the positive side, this means that communal relationships are possible, because *we* may will them into existence.

"But" (the other part of the answer) the extent to which we have such a will is substantially influenced by our social location. On the negative side, then, is the fact that we live in a society that is not supportive of community. This means that not only are durable relationships difficult to maintain but the will to commit ourselves to such relationships is similarly lacking. The question is, How can we become committed to relationships when the spirit is weak?

To make the intimate community a reality in the modern world, we will need teamwork. We will, in the first place, need the help of Christ. The fundamental problem remains sin. We cannot possibly deal effectively (over the long run) with the social or personal manifestations of sin until we have grappled effectively with sin itself. The work that Christ has already accomplished must be "permitted" to take root in our lives. We must remember that, in the end, only God will be able to overcome the Evil One. And it is against the Evil One that we are here doing battle.

Having Christ on our side (or, more accurately, being on *his* side) is only the first step, however. It assures us of having the right coaching staff and of gaining the ultimate victory (to stretch the analogy), but it does not obviate the need to play the game. Some Christians, unfortunately, forget this point, while others forget the need to be on the team at all. As a result, the church seems to be forever divided between those who say, "Christ is the answer" and those who retort, "What is the question?" The experience of being born again is perceived as an end-all or as irrelevant to the problems of the "real world." But it is neither. It is rather a rebirth—a miraculous chance to *live* again.

The question remains: How do we live the new life in the midst of modernity? More precisely, how do we live as members of the intimate community in the context of modernity? We do it, quite simply, with other Christians. Individuals, whether they are Christians or not, cannot solve the problem of relationships. This is a truism, I know, but one that bears repeating.

I alone cannot create a genuine community. Individuals living in the context of modernity may have the desire to found durable family relationships, but they lack the social support—and thus the will—to carry it off. This is why families disintegrate, even though individuals may desperately want them to remain intact. This is why even Christian families disintegrate, even though the Lord of the universe commands it otherwise.

The *mutual commitments* of a number of Christians, however, *can* solve the problem of relationships. Despite the problems inherent in modernity—in spite of the problems of choice, insecurity, self-gratification, and other-directed fantasy—the intimate community can prevail if it is able to muster the common commitments of its members.

Why is this so? Why is it that common commitments can make such a difference? From a sociological perspective, reciprocal relational commitments are a most intriguing phenomenon. They are one of the points at which seemingly individual behavior patterns come together to form social structures and social forces. Simply put, when a number of people commit themselves to one another, they become a very powerful group— one capable of exercising a great deal of influence over its members (for good as well as for ill). The deeper the commitment, the more powerful the social bond. In a sense, mutual commitments transform a collection of individuals into a social force.

For the family, this means that the intimate community is possible even if the host environment (modernity) is not especially supportive. The social bond of mutual commitments is strong. It is capable of helping its members live up to their communal ideals as well as to ward off countervailing social influences. In the short run (one generation) this occurs primarily through mutual accountability—simple reminders to flagging members of their original commitment to the community. Over time, however, values can be developed that support the objectives of the community, and traditions can be established to enhance community values. When that takes place, genuine community can blossom, even in the desert of modernity.

COMMITMENTS OF ANOTHER KIND

But what kind of mutual commitments are required to establish the intimate community? Not the modern kind, we can be sure. They cannot be based purely on feelings, nor can they play second fiddle to success fantasies or the myths of self- or other-family fulfillment. Such commitments are not commitments at all. They are mere contingency clauses in a contractual relationship of convenience.

By mutual commitments, I mean "covenants of foreverness"—the promise to do whatever love requires for the sake of the other, forever. Such commitments endure because they are robust, and they are strong because they are rooted in love. "Love is patient and kind; love is not jealous or boastful; it is not arrogant or rude. Love does not insist on its own way; it is not irritable or resentful; it does not rejoice at wrong, but rejoices in the right. Love bears all things, believes all things, hopes all things, endures all things" (1 Corinthians 13:4–8 RSV).

Covenants of foreverness bear and endure. They are not provisional. They do not say, "I will stick with you as long as you are wonderful, wise, and socially acceptable." They depend neither on the curvature of one's anatomy nor on the bent of one's personality. They put up with pain. They endure under sorrow. They hold up under the strain of critical comments. They tolerate unexpected eccentricities. They bear the weight of unfulfilled dreams. They restrain the urge of untapped passions. They abide the weak, the powerless, the frail—the ones who would otherwise be homeless.

Covenants of foreverness believe and hope. They affirm the value of dependable relationships. They assume, even in the most difficult of circumstances, that there is merit in honoring relational commitments. They trust in the long haul, knowing that happiness is more than a momentary feeling, that joy is more than the scratching of an itch. They believe in one another—not in their perfection, but in their worth; not in their accomplishments, but in their ability to accomplish. They hope for the best—not because they are blind to weakness, but because they see possibilities where others dare not even grope.

Covenants of foreverness never end. Where there are choices, they will cease. Where there are other possibilities, they will pass away. Where there is success, it will come to nothing. Every job, every experience, every curve, every feeling—all will turn to vapor. "I became great and surpassed all who were before me in Jerusalem .... Whatever my eyes desired I did not keep from them; I kept my heart from no pleasure .... Then I considered all that my hands had done .... all was vanity and a striving after wind" (Ecclesiastes 2:9-11 RSV).

Only "faith, hope, love abide, these three; but the greatest of these is love" (1 Corinthians 13:13 RSV).

CONCLUSION

He had a brother. You know—the pastor? The one who had taken flight from a successful church, a loving family, and a fifteen-year marriage, in search of another possibility. He had an older brother.

The older brother was not like the younger. For one thing, he was terribly average. He was a mediocre student, able to get through the local state college, but that's about all. His athletic skills were not substantial either. He could play sandlot baseball without embarrassment, for example, but could never letter in a varsity sport. Socially he managed, but he was far from adept. He stuttered a little and seemed uncomfortable around unfamiliar faces. He did not initiate new friendships easily, but he rarely lost old ones either. About the only thing he did well was float. He was incredibly buoyant.

After graduation from college, he took a job as an accountant with a rather common firm and married a girl of like description. Everyone agreed that his career choice was, far and away, the superior decision. His wife married him on the rebound from another relationship, more out of spite than affection. As a result, she never considered him quite up to her level and felt a bit cheated by the fates. Within a year of their marriage, she began drinking to excess and engaging in semidiscreet extramarital affairs. On one of her trysts, she was involved in an automobile accident that left her stomach badly scarred, and her future childless. From that point forward, her life was characterized by a series of lovers and extended bouts with alcoholism.

It was during the younger brother's flight to freedom that the two brothers got together—for the first time in years. The younger was moving with his girlfriend to an apartment in a nearby town and, knowing no one in the area and needing assistance, asked his brother to give him a hand. So the older brother took a day off from work and helped his brother clean floors, paint walls, and move furniture. It was good to be together again and, in an odd sort of way, the two felt closer than they had for years.

That evening, the younger took the older out to eat, a reward of sorts for his beneficence and charity. As the night progressed, the younger brother began to unload about his years as a "successful" pastor. He

talked of the incessant pressure—to come up with a
sizzling sermon each week, to be creative on demand,
to encourage others when he felt depressed, to thank
church members for their "suggestions" when he felt
like punching them in the nose, to have the perfect
family, and to be a role model, not only to his kids,
but to an entire congregation. He talked as well about
his wife, who was so perfect that he couldn't figure
out whether to worship her or hate her. In the end,
he concluded she was perfectly boring, and that's
when he decided he had to get out; he could not
handle professional pressure and personal boredom in
tandem. Especially not after he met Ruth . . . .

As he regurgitated his tale of woe and relief, it
eventually began to dawn on him that his older
brother's life was also less than a happy story. Indeed,
while he had been stuck with the pressures of success
and the boredom of perfection, his brother was stuck
with professional mediocrity and a marital disaster.
The contrast made him feel uneasy, and so he began
to ask his brother a series of probing questions—about
his job, his hobbies, and his wife. Of his job, the
older brother talked a little. Of his hobbies, he talked
a lot. Of his wife, he would say not a word.

But it was of the wife the younger could not stop
thinking. And the more he ruminated, the more angry
and incredulous he became. Finally, in the middle of
one of the older brother's fishing yarns, the younger
could hold it in no longer.

"Why don't you just leave her?" he blurted, without
finesse or his usual charm.

"What?" came the surprised voice of the older
brother.

"Why don't you simply walk out on your wife?"
repeated the younger. "She's no good! Everybody
knows that. She drinks too much. She cheats on you.
Why waste your life on her? You're too good for her!"

The older looked at the younger for a moment, as one who did not understand. Then, in silence, he slipped out of his chair and walked slowly out of the restaurant.

The eyes of the younger followed his brother— through the door and as far into the darkness as his vision would permit. There they stayed transfixed until his head could bear their weight no longer. Then, sobbing, he dropped his head onto his arms.

fifteen / Questioning the Judgments of the Modern Family

Mutual commitments are the lifeblood of the intimate community. With them, the communal family is a modern possibility; without them, it is unlikely to withstand the onslaught of modernity.

Two factors will play a crucial role in the ability of family members to maintain their commitments. The first is a well-thought-out approach to the family, consciously designed to undergird the intimate community. The second is a thorough understanding of the values of modernity and a willingness to question modern judgments that run counter to the needs and commitments of the intimate community. The first will be discussed in chapter 16; the latter is the task that now confronts us.

QUESTION: MUST WE MOVE?

If mobility is a significant factor in the development and pervasive influence of modernity, then we must (once again) question its value. In doing so, however, we need to keep two points in mind. First, being immobile does not negate the influence of a mobile society. Whether or not we change our place of residence, we will still be bombarded with societal values engendered by mobility. Immobility, therefore, is not an easy answer to the problem of modernity. Nor, in the second place, is immobility always the "correct" answer. There clearly are times when we should move—when the answer to the question "Must we move?" will be yes. Those whom God has called into foreign missions, for example, will need to move, as will many of those called to participate in politics, medicine, education, social service, etc. Once again, immobility is no simple cure for the vicissitudes of modern family life.

In part, this is because we *live* in a mobile society. To the extent that Christians are called to permeate and transform society (and I strongly believe they are—salt, light, and all that), they cannot all remain geographically transfixed. Too many occupations would go unattended; too many people would never be confronted by the mercy or message of the Good News. The apostles were certainly not immobile, nor was Jesus, nor necessarily ought we to be. Christians are not called to immobility.

Nevertheless, if we desire to be part of the intimate community, we must question the modern compulsion to move. The simple fact is that mobility is a killer of community; it destroys some relationships and makes all others volitional. Nothing reminds the individual of his power over relationships—to pick and choose and discard—so much as mobility. And nothing so readily undermines the traditions on which community thrives.

For the family, the most troublesome aspect of mobility is its effect on relationships outside the nuclear family. Although a change of residence is often a strain for parents and children, it just as often draws them closer together. After all, when a family moves to a new town, other family members are sometimes the only significant people left in their lives. Geographical mobility, however, is deadly on extrafamily relationships—with friends, neighbors, grandparents, cousins, church members, and so on. Not only does it put distance between the family and such folk, but it makes choice king and greatly erodes the constraining influence of community relationships.

For example, if my family moves from Upland to Miami, we are immediately faced with the need to choose new relationships. This not only makes such relationships a matter of personal taste but also creates a self-interest perspective toward these same affiliations. That is, I pick new friends for my pleasure, not for my benefit. These are "feel good" relationships, not ones that prod, push, critique, or annoy, much less support in times of trouble. As a result, from the moment I settle in Miami, the only semicommunal relationships left in my life are those of the nuclear family. Presto: the self-fulfilling family.

Moreover, the old relationships we left in Upland will immediately lose a great deal of their power as well. They become "rhetoric relationships" based purely on verbal communication (letters, telephone, intermittent visits, etc.). Rhetoric relationships can be extremely enjoyable, of course, but they are hardly communal. The problem is that in such relationships all experiences are passed through the filter of reflection and rationalization. We explain how "awful" or how "wonderful" things are, and our audience responds accordingly. There is nothing wrong with such relationships; indeed, they can be quite helpful—clinical psychologists make a good living off of our need for rhetoric relationships. However, they are a far cry from relationships based on the give-and-take of daily life. They are contrived relationships, not communities.

The point of all this, I trust, is clear. I have no interest in undermining rhetoric relationships (which I enjoy in abundance) or feel-good friendships (ditto). In the modern world, we ought to be thankful just to have relationships, rhetorical or otherwise. But these are not communal relationships and we must not delude ourselves into thinking that they are adequate to meet the human need for community. There is no escaping the fact that, for those who acknowledge the need for durable relationships, mobility is a significant problem.

This fact raises an important question: If mobility is a genuine problem on the one hand, but often necessary on the other (as per the first paragraph of this section), what do we do? How can we reconcile the need to move in some circumstances (e.g., the missionary) with our concern about the effects of mobility on community? While proscriptions must await the next chapter, we do get some insight into this problem from Paul's first letter to the Corinthians.

In 1 Corinthians 7 Paul advises the unmarried to remain single "in view of the present distress" (7:26 RSV); "I want you to be free from anxieties," says Paul, so you can concentrate on "how to please the Lord" and not have divided interests (7:32–34 RSV). These verses, unfortunately, have been badly treated over the years, some thinking they imply a dualism between God's interests and the worldly interests of the family, and others believing they prove the superiority of singleness. Both interpretations are flatly contradicted by the whole of Scripture, however, and richly deserve our inattention. A much more congruent interpretation, and one that is relevant to our concern here, is that the apostle recognizes that marriage entails responsibilities, and these responsibilities restrict the married person's freedom. Therefore, given Paul's concern about "the present distress" (the details about which we are ignorant), it would be easier to devote oneself to the tasks of the church if one were not married—if one did not have to be anxious about a spouse and children.

Sound advice. Singleness can be both a gift and an advantage in certain situations. The church, throughout much of its history, has recognized that fact, some parts even requiring singleness of the clergy. Regardless of what one thinks about such a requirement, modern Christians clearly want no part of anything remotely resembling a limitation on their conjugal rights. Therefore, we get married (if we want to) and then do whatever else we imagine God desires of us. If that means dragging a nuclear family all over God's good earth, then so be it. Marriage is our right. Mobility is our right. And, in modernity, rights must be exercised.

The apostle Paul recognized something many moderns do not: choices entail responsibilities. If we want to do certain kinds of things, we may need to avoid marriage; if we want marriage, we may need to give up doing certain things. Those of us who are married are not as free to move as our single counterparts. At the very least, we ought to move our families only after a great deal of input from God and the Christian community. Only then will we have the guts to ask ourselves that archaic question: Must we move? God grant us the fortitude to periodically say no.

QUESTION: HOW VALUABLE IS THE CHOICE?

Mobility, of course, is only one of many choices modernity presents to the modern family. Others include options about marriage, marriage partners, courtship patterns, governance models, residency patterns, sexual behavior, children, and marital longevity, not to mention a multitude of day-to-day decisions unknown to the ancients. Living within the modern family (as well as outside) is to exist under an avalanche of choices, each one theoretically designed to make life just a bit more wonderful.

But, do they make life more wonderful? The honest answer, I think, is "Sometimes they do." Most adults laboring within the modern family can look back at their lives and think of numerous decisions that were, indeed, wonderful. Spouses chosen, as well as some rejected possibilities; living arrangements that improved life considerably; techniques of intimacy that liberated libidos; models of authority that relieved burdens of responsibility or, possibly, oppression. Without a doubt, some choices open to the modern family are immensely rewarding.

Others, if we are honest, have not worked out so well. The spouse chosen on the basis of availability may have been worse than no spouse at all. The house chosen for its exterior beauty may have been riddled with termites or located in a poor school district. The new governance model may have created more oppression than it relieved. New sexual possibilities may have stimulated expectations more than passions, leading to failure rather than delight. Like the list of rewarding choices, the catalog of debacles is endless.

The question is, of course, how can we distinguish between rewarding and disastrous decisions? At least, that is the modern question. Indeed, I would argue that "making the right decision" is a modern preoccupation. Stroll through a bookstore sometime (Christian or otherwise) and count the number of volumes devoted to making the right decision—about lover, spouse, sex, money, vacation, fashion, residence, authority, whatever. It is not even unknown to find books devoted to making good decisions about "community"! We moderns are consumed with the desire to select the best option and are willing to invest heavily in the promise of successful decision-making techniques. Such an approach assumes that it is possible to confront the problem of choice rationally and construct one's life around the best possible choices to achieve the best possible life.

This assumption contains an element of truth but is substantially flawed. The truth is, we can make reasonably good decisions between *known* options under *known* circumstances. However, given our finitude, we can never know all available options, nor understand the circumstances surrounding those options, nor predict the consequences of choosing one of those options. Moreover, given our sinful condition, we cannot even trust the information we are given by others, permeated as it is with prejudice and selfish ambition. Add to this the fact that our own decisions are similarly suspect because of human depravity, and we discover how extraordinarily difficult it is to rationally construct the "best possible life." (Also implied in this is the reason the human sciences have failed to live up to positivistic expectations.)

Interestingly, the choices we are best equipped to make are not about lifestyle but about life virtues. It is the moral choice that comes to us most clearly, not choices about what will make us the happiest people. Even though the problems of finitude and sin affect moral decisions (as well as others), and even though we find it difficult to live up to our own normative standards, nevertheless, if the desire is present, moral choices are less complicated than "happiness decisions."

Take the simple matter of eating a candy bar, for example. Is it a good "happiness decision" to eat a candy bar? That is an easy question to answer only if one dislikes candy bars. Otherwise, it is very difficult indeed. The candy bar might taste delicious, and that might make me happy. However, it will also add unwanted ounces, and that could make me unhappy in the long run. Moreover, the candy might upset my stomach or raise my blood sugar level (the latter possibility could be considered good or bad depending on a variety of variables). It might even cause cancer. The point is, there are a great many unknowns about eating a candy bar, all of which make the happiness decision a very complicated one.

Stealing a candy bar, however, is an altogether different kind of matter. Within the Judeo-Christian tradition (along with many others), it is clearly wrong— morally wrong. One may, of course, decide that it is worth doing for some reason, but not because the decision is morally murky. For example, I may say to myself, "If I steal the candy bar, I can give it to my son, and this will please him as well as me; therefore, it is not a 'bad' thing for me to steal this particular candy bar at this time in my life." This kind of reasoning enables me to feel good because it seems as though I am stealing for higher moral purposes. In fact, however, I am making an immoral choice for purely utilitarian purposes. Here it is not the moral decision that is difficult or complex. The difficulty resides in using "happiness values" to make a moral decision. Moreover, since happiness decisions are almost always ambiguous (Will the candy bar *really* be good for my son?), mixing them into a moral decision not only clouds the moral issue but also makes the decision more difficult.

The point, however, is not simply that we moderns are enamored with "happiness decisions" (though we are), nor that such decisions are very complicated and ambiguous (which they are), but that making such choices fundamentally undermines the intimate community. When we are constantly in search of *the* house, or *the* governance structure, or *the* church—according the happiness values of modernity—relationships are discarded or treated as secondary, traditions wither, and our vision becomes utilitarian. We will not long think of the family as a source of stability in our lives if it is regularly subjected to choice.

Does this mean that we should refrain altogether from making choices about sex, governance, residence, etc.? Certainly not. Good choices need to be made and, in modernity, must be made. But we need to keep in mind that such choices are not nearly as promising as modernity claims, nor are they a guarantee of happiness. Moreover, if they are not settled readily—if they are persistently asked and renegotiated—they will effect the eventual demise of the intimate community. Given such stakes, it would be well for us to remain skeptical of the value of choice.

QUESTION: FOR WHOM IS THE SELF-FULFILLING FAMILY FULFILLING?

The family ideal that many of us hold—the one most often cultivated in the church and elsewhere—is the self-fulfilling family. It contains a mother, a father, and a few minor children (along with a cat or dog), all residing in one home and all "totally fulfilled" by the family. It is the modern family ideal.

The self-fulfilling family maintains its place of esteem for good reason. It has the dual benefit of fitting into the needs of modern society and guarding against many of the less desirable aspects of modernity. In other words, the self-fulfilling family is a structural adaptation to modernity (despite employing "traditional family values" as its legitimation and *raison d'etre*). Being small and self-contained, it is mobile and readily adaptable to different environments. Unencumbered by external relationships, family members are free to move as modern economic circumstances require. On the other hand, the self-fulfilling family decries many of the values of modernity. It abhors the temptation of other possibilities (i.e., the modern promise of fulfillment through another relationship), for example, and it resists those modern influences (e.g., sexual libertarianism) that threaten nuclear family relationships. For this reason, it is often assumed to be the Christian ideal.

A more Christian view of the self-fulfilling family, however, is that it is at best one possible adaptation to modernity and, at worst, one of its primary problems. It may not be the most malevolent structure in the world (it is certainly better than total "family-lessness"), but it is hardly the ideal solution to the problem of community. For one thing, it is so narrowly defined and its membership so exclusive that it leaves many people out of the modern family— widows, unmarried adults, the elderly, etc. And yet, some of these who are excluded are precisely the ones who need the security and aid of family relationships. In ancient China, the elderly were given the right to wear yellow, the color of royalty; in modernity we often find it difficult to tolerate their presence in the family. In the light of the fifth commandment, such contrasts are by no means purely academic. They raise serious questions about the adequacy of the modern family, as well as the level of commitment of those who seek to find total fulfillment there.

Second, by attempting the art of self-satisfaction, the self-fulfilling family tends to break down community bonds that lie beyond its purview. The neighborhood, the church, the town, and the nation all suffer as a result, becoming secondary communities at best, and more than likely of trivial importance. How often does one hear the statement "Family is my first priority" used as an excuse to abrogate responsibility to church and neighbor? While Christians can debate the relative merits of these various communities, they cannot debate their rights to survival (they *all* have them) nor the family's right to be worshiped (an idolatrous claim). The tragedy, of course, is that nonfamily communities also suffer the effects of modernity. They too have their communal bonds under attack. When the family is played against these other communities, it does battle with one of its own kind and, in the long run, undermines its own claims to legitimacy. We cannot generate community in one area by destroying it in others.

Third, because the self-fulfilling family is a self-contained, self-satisfying arrangement, it is easily relocated. Thus if I get a better job offer in Nashville, it is relatively easy for me to justify the move. After all, the family will stay together; I will be making more money; and we can buy a better house, live in a more exclusive neighborhood, and enjoy one another more fully. If one's life revolves totally around the nuclear family, the nuclear family becomes the only consideration worth taking into account. Such an approach to life not only reinforces modernistic mobility patterns (hurting the family in the long run), but it is also a thinly veiled form of hedonism. Almost any expenditure, any extravagance, can be justified in the name of the self-fulfilling family.

Finally, even for those who are assumed to be the beneficiaries of the self-fulfilling family (married adults and their children), there are significant risks. If the self-fulfilling family were the fortress of its pretensions—if it really were an adequate source of protection from modernity—then it might be a genuinely attractive option. Unfortunately, it offers little protection from modern choices or the seduction of "other possibilities." Such allurements, which might entice a husband or wife out of the family, are especially dangerous to the self-fulfilling family. Once it collapses, the self-fulfilling fantasy is over. Suddenly one finds oneself outside the family and terribly alone. And where are the other relationships—with neighbor, fellow Christians, or extended-family members—that might offer support and see one through the difficult times? Gone—with the self-fulfilling family.

QUESTION: AT WHAT PRICE THE OTHER-DIRECTED FANTASY?

With all its inherent weaknesses, the self-fulfilling family is at least a family. It is an attempt at community, however ill-informed or aberrant it may be. Things could be worse. We could find ourselves on a quest for an illusion without the slightest possibility of communal fulfillment.

Throughout this book I have written about the modern predisposition to choose. Because my primary concern has been to explore its effect on the community, I have stressed the negative consequences of choicism for those who live among us—husbands, wives, children, grandparents, singles, and the weak—those who fear and feel the effects of "other possibilities." Let me conclude this chapter, however, not with a discussion of the communal effects of the other-directed fantasy, but with a look at its impact on the self. How does it affect *me*?

The "me" in this case represents the strong members of the intimate community. They are the individualists among us who spurn the need for present relationships in the hope of finding other, more exciting ones. Perhaps they even dream of being freed from family ties altogether—of the possibility of living their lives as they desire, without the encumbrance of others' values or needs or relational dependencies. It may not be the call of other relationships that propels them, but the need to flee the weak.

"Me" is an appropriate name for this person, since most of us who inhabit the modern world have felt such pangs and longings. We have felt them because we are sinners who are motivated by self-interest and the hope of a more pleasurable existence. We have felt them because we live in a society where they are cultivated en masse, dressed fit to kill, and served as the Last Supper. We have felt them because we sinners have shaped society.

We have felt these pangs and longings also because we moderns are the strong of the world. Wealthy beyond the Ethiopian child's wildest imaginings, we are the ones who have the economic power to shape our world in our own image. With power comes the possibility of change. With the possibility of change comes the belief that things could be "better"—not for the world as a whole (to which we pay lip service), but for me in particular (for which we pay dearly). Whether the stage is international or familial, the strong have the same temptations. And we are the strong.

The question is, How fulfilling are these other possibilities? At this point I think we must be honest with ourselves and admit to the potentiality of their giving us pleasure. It will not do to slough off "other possibilities" as mere insanities, in which we would be crazy to participate. One cannot fight for truth with a lie. The fact is, God created us as material beings. We enjoy exploring the full range of our senses because God infused us with their delights. If there is genuine pleasure in tasting a new flavor of ice cream or a novel cuisine, why should we doubt similar satisfaction with a new relationship? We should not.

It is not immediate gratification we must contest, but the dream of the abundant life. The illusion is not the promise of pleasure, but the expectation of fulfillment—the notion that all my wants and needs will be met if only I am able to escape my present relational circumstances and replace them with new ones. Here it is that we confront the lie.

For one thing, all pleasures are short-lived. We know that, all of us, but we often live otherwise. If sometime in the morning I set my sights on lobster thermidor for dinner, from that time on nothing else will do. The lobster becomes ever more appetizing, and whatever I have in my cupboard (canned tuna, no doubt) is devalued accordingly. Once I have devoured the thermidor, however, my desire for it ebbs, not because lobster is no longer desirable, but because my appetite is satisfied and I have other needs besides food. All pleasures, including the pleasurable aspects of human relationships, are short-lived because each is only one pleasure among many, only one part of a full life. We crave only what we do not possess. Once we possess it, our cravings turn to other objectives. What this means, then, is that the potential joys attendant on the other-directed fantasy depend, for their very existence, on our *not* achieving them.

There is a good chance, moreover, that the coveted new relationship, when once we achieve it, will be incredibly like the old. It is often reported, for example, that people who divorce tend to find a second spouse similar to the first. Why? Because they are still attracted by the same kind of person, with the same kind of kinks and personality traits. Put in other language, they liked a great deal about their former spouse, more than they would ever have admitted at the time.

The new relationship, however, will not only be like the old in positive qualities, it will also contain many of its undesirable aspects. Many of the same irritants and frustrations, for example, will be a part of the other-directed fantasy, once we attain it. We will still be annoyed by people who chat in the morning, fail to keep the lawn manicured, work until the wee hours of the evening, or wear holy underwear and a countenance to match. The reason, of course, is that *we* are the same person. In contrast to our hopes, we do not become new creatures in new relationships. We are not "born again" by other human beings, no matter how wonderful, no matter how redemptive their spirit. To believe in such possibilities is not only a form of idolatry (one to which our society is especially prone), it is also to bear the burden of false expectations; to believe a lie.

Finally, for the strong to assume the right to escape present family relationships in search of new ones is both arrogant and naïve. It is arrogant because it forgets the time when the one who is now strong was once weak. Who has come into this world on his own? Who has passed through the first few years of life unaided by the helping hands of others? Who has carved out his niche in society with only his own chisel? Who could have made it without those who were strong and willing to use their strength to aid the weak? Who could have survived if the strong, in their moment of weakness, had assumed the right to escape?

It is also naïve to assume that right. For who among us is strong forever?

sixteen / Toward the Intimate Community

We come finally to the most precarious part of our journey, where detail replaces catholicity, and theory gives way to praxis. It is precarious, not because practical suggestions are difficult to make, but because they have no definite target. Those who read these pages are largely unknown to me; and yet suggestions are not for unknowns, but for real people who have precise needs in the midst of particular circumstances. So how does one give advice to an imperceptible audience?

Very carefully. In the pages to follow, I want to lay out some general guidelines for those who wish to cultivate the intimate community, even among the thistles of modernity. These guidelines are not etched in stone, nor are they guaranteed to produce results. Mutual commitments are the goal—not clever techniques or foolproof designs. No technique will assure a durable relationship, and no design can restrain the fool. Especially the modern fool. But suggestions can be helpful to those of willing disposition and discerning judgment. It is for these that we must continue our trek, even on the shifting sands of "advice."

Laying Hold of Present Circumstances

Many who read these pages find little satisfaction in their present family circumstances. When judged against the standards of the traditional family, few modern families merit commendation. Even by existing standards, many within the modern family feel like failures. Few people plan on a divorce, for example, yet many (most?) will experience its effects. The majority of us, moreover, are estranged from some members of our family, whether spouse, children, parents, or other close relatives. Indeed, rare is the contemporary soul who escapes the ravages of modern "choicism."

Under such conditions, it is important to get beyond the facts of history (which cannot be changed) and get on with the possibilities of the day. Brooding over past relational failures will not result in community. Rather, in the modern era, it will only convince a person of the impossibility of community. Failure is all around us; it is part and parcel of modern existence. If we look to our own circumstances for hope, we will be sorely disappointed.

Nor will it do much good to bear incessantly the yoke of guilt over family breakdowns. One of my fears in writing this book is that it will produce more guilt than communal intent. Guilt, of course, is not a bad

248

thing—provided it results from an awareness of sin and leads to contrition and reformation. But guilt over sins forgiven, or never committed, is a tool of the Evil One. It leads only to despair and insecurity, immobilizing the spirit and inhibiting the will to overcome.

But "overcoming" is precisely what we in the modern family must do if we are to participate in the intimate community. It will not take place, however, if we are either vexed by social circumstances or paralyzed by personal failures. It depends, instead, on our willingness to lay aside anxieties about what might have been and to thank God for the relationships we now possess—regardless of how partial or imperfect they might be. In the modern world, the intimate community must begin, not with despair over directions once taken, but with a readiness to lay hold of present circumstances.

An Enlarged View of "Family"

J. B. Phillips once penned a powerful little book entitled *Your God Is Too Small* (New York: Macmillan, n.d.). In it he makes the argument that the modern conception of God does not correspond to reality. We think of him, not as the Lord of creation, but the "Grand Old Man" or "Managing Director" or even "Resident Policeman." As a result, our lives are less than they could be because our conception of the God we worship is less than it should be.

There is a sense, I think, in which the same argument could be made with regard to the family. The modern ideal of the family is a very limited one. It contains a parent or two and possibly a couple of children—nothing more. A group of three or four (or possibly five), cleaving to one another in an attempt to be a total family. In effect, we have limited our conception of the family to those who live with us. The modern *household* has become the *family*. No one else is permitted to encroach on the sacred turf of the family.

Unlike the modern conception of God, however, our expectations of the modern family are very high. Indeed, we expect this minute cadre to be totally fulfilling. It is required to meet all of our emotional needs, to take care of every financial obligation, and to be our only source of genuine relationships. If it is functioning properly, it ought to be a wellspring of inspiration also, amusing and entertaining at all times. In short, it is supposed to be everything to everybody, in spite of the limited number of "bodies" available to do the things that must be done. It is little wonder, then, that we in the modern family who are forever expecting complete fulfillment in family are in danger of slipping off to other-directed fantasy. We either try to live up to this dream of the totally fulfilling family—and thereby ignore the needs of those who are not a part of it—or, if we sense failure, are seduced into believing that total fulfillment might be possible, if only we had the "right" family.

There are, of course, no easy solutions to this problem. The modern family is contoured to fit the needs of modern society. Those who attempt to develop a different kind of family, therefore, will struggle not only against the modern conception of the family but against modern social facts as well. Such a struggle will require more than creativity. It will take a great deal of intestinal fortitude.

If we have such resolve, however, then our conceptions can make a difference. And the first thing we must do, I believe, is change our perception of family. In particular, I think it is crucial that we expand our view of what constitutes "our" family. Of one thing I am convinced: we will not get off the trolley of the self- and other-fulfilling family until we have laid to rest the notion that the family consists only of parents and minor children. Such a family may be good for modernity, but it is lousy for people. It encourages greed, ignores the weak, and fosters fantasy. Most important, it makes durable relationships almost impossible.

The question is, How should we conceive of the family? If the nuclear family is inadequate, what is adequate? What should constitute the intimate community? While there can be no definitive answer to this question (it is neither a biblical nor a cultural imperative), let me suggest a helpful rule of thumb: "Try not to lose a family member." That is, regardless of how one presently defines one's family, one should try not to allow future developments (mobility, disinterest, disgust, whatever) to sever the family tie. Regardless of how physically removed one may become, how psychologically distant one may sometimes feel, one should try not to give up on a family member. In saying this, I am not making a judgment concerning where family members ought to live, how often they ought to get together, what the lines of authority ought to be, or how family members ought to relate to one another. I am merely asserting that, if at all possible, we should not let someone slip out of our conception of the family.

Though this rule may appear innocuous, consider its implications. Let us say that I am a child in a family consisting of a father, a mother, and two children (i.e., a modern family). At that point, such would be my entire family. As I grow up, however, my "family" will expand. If I choose to marry and have children, if my sister chooses to marry and have children, if either of our childrens' children chooses to marry and have children—in all of these cases, my "family" will grow with each additional spouse or offspring.

Note, however, what happens to the families of my children: they begin with a family that includes not only parents and siblings but also first cousins and uncles and aunts. Moreover, if their spouses have a similar conception of their family, at the time they marry they will inherit an entire additional set of parents, siblings, cousins, and aunts and uncles. For my grandchildren, the family involves grandparents, parents, siblings, first and second cousins, and aunts and uncles. If and when they marry, the possibility exists that this group would once again be doubled.

Clearly the problem with this "rule of thumb" is not that it is innocuous, but that it is far too radical. If followed ruthlessly, it would result in a family of unimaginable proportions. Before pursuing the implications of this idea, therefore, let me briefly specify the limits within which it is offered. First, I am not assuming that there is an ideal extended-family size. How far this rule of thumb is carried, it seems to me, depends on the individual doing the measuring. Heaven has yet to reveal the precise dimensions of the proper family, and I will not attempt to improve on heaven's silence. My guess is that, given the constraints of modernity, few people will be able to carry it beyond the realm of first cousins. But even that would be a vast improvement over contemporary standards. The point is not to define the maximum size of the intimate community, but to ensure that it extends beyond the modern family household.

Second, by saying that the family should extend beyond the nuclear family, I am not assuming an equality of responsibilities across all expanded-family relationships. That is, just because my nephew is now a part of my family does not mean I have the same responsibilities toward him that I do toward my own son. I do not. My duties as father are different from my duties as uncle, and this does not change within the expanded family. In sociological language, my roles as father, husband, uncle, child, cousin, or whatever, remain functionally distinct in the expanded family. Moreover, some relationships have priority over others; the relationship of husband and wife, for example, takes precedence over the parent-child relationship (see Genesis 2:24). And although the expanded family enlarges the borders of the family concept, it does not blur family responsibilities. Indeed, it ought to make them more precise.

Finally, I trust it is clear that I am not attempting to proscribe a particular family living arrangement. When some people think of the extended family, they immediately envision a very large home with three or four families living under one roof. Although some cultures do handle the issue of residence in that manner, and though some in our culture may wish to do the same, it is by no means necessary or even desirable to do so. While proximity is an extremely important issue, the appropriate distance between members of the expanded family is a matter for prayer and familial deliberation. It is certainly not something to be determined by this or any other author.

The Consequence of Expansion

If the expanded family is merely an expanded *conception* of the family, without absolute definitions of size or residence, will it really make any difference? Can anything significant result from it? Although such a change may seem trivial, it is nothing of the sort. Three consequences of the expanded family are, in fact, quite revolutionary.

First, an expanded family retards the drive toward mobility. Putting it crudely, moving from place to place is much more difficult if one has to consider its impact on a family of twelve adults and sixteen children (for example) rather than two adults and two children. Suddenly, it is no longer just a matter of mom and dad, sitting down to calculate whether or not a new job will pay more or allow them to live in a better neighborhood or bring them more prestige. Now they must also calculate the cost of separating themselves from other family members. In other words, they must weigh the benefits of mobility against its relational costs. They are not free to think that, with mobility, their family can remain unaffected. It cannot. This does not mean, of course, that they will choose to stay put. Some will leave; indeed, some should leave. But none will do so without knowing profoundly the price they have paid.

Second, the expanded family frees the nuclear family from its obligation to meet all family needs. When someone is having financial difficulty, it offers a very practical form of social security. When someone is sick, it offers hands to cook, care, and comfort. When someone is in despair, it offers ears to listen and eyes to cry. When someone is at his or her moment of triumph, it offers voices to rejoice and hands to clap. It serves, as well, to remind the triumphant of their finitude. In other words, the expanded family replaces the fantasy of the totally fulfilling nuclear family with the reality of helpful hands and regular people. It is a simple reality, to be sure, but one that the myths of modernity are unable to cope with.

Finally, the expanded family leaves no room for exclusivity. Once one's conception of the family stretches beyond spouse and children, it immediately moves out of the purview of personal choice. I may select my spouse. With my spouse I may decide whether and when to have children. But I do not choose my parents, brothers and sisters, their spouses, or their children. In other words, the expanded family includes many members whose presence results from the choices of others. If such people are a part of my conception of what family is, then my family is neither the sole product of my imagination nor under my sovereign control. The practical implication is that I am no longer free to exclude people from the intimate community because they might be a burden to me or because they fail to live up to my standards of the ideal family member. The widow and the widower, the single and the married, the poor and the successful, the deviant and the model citizen—all are within the borders of my family. I have no grounds to exclude them.

It is its inclusive nature that makes the family unique and, I believe, irreplaceable. Some have argued that the local church should substitute for the extended family—that, with the breakdown of the modern family, the only alternative is the cultivation of Christian communities that function as families. I believe such thinking is dangerous and seriously flawed. The essential nature of a church is exclusive; the family, however, is fundamentally inclusive. The church is made up of those who are disciples of Christ only; the family includes the heretic as well as the holy. Both communities are necessary, but neither should attempt to usurp the responsibilities of the other.

Because the expanded family is inclusive, it forces us to come face to face with the whole of life. The expanded family is not tame. Within its domain we will confront the beautiful and the ugly, birth and death, foolishness and wisdom, sinner and saint, love and hatred. Although its relationships will at times cost us great pain and grief, it will also confront us with reality—not a reality "out there" that we can ignore or neglect, but a reality permanently attached to our being. Living in the real world is not easy. That is why we moderns exercise so many choices in an effort to escape it. But it is neither to ease nor escape to which we have been called. It is to the world for whom Christ died.

A Trilogy of Concern

We ought to be clear about one thing: modernity is comfortable with the mini-family. An industrialized, urbanized society—especially in Western form—will not easily accommodate the expanded family. The demands of the workplace as well as the needs of the market encourage (some would say, necessitate) a mobile, free-floating population. Most of us, moreover, are living in mini-families, aspects of which we enjoy and appreciate. Breaking out of the modern mold, therefore, will not be easy nor, at times, pleasurable.

But by the grace of God and because of his image in us, we can go against the grain of society. Indeed, we can not only go against it, we can substantially change it. That, I know, is an audacious statement for a sociologist to make. Yet I believe it because the Word of God proclaims its truth. I believe it too because his people, when rooted in his Word and enabled by his Spirit, have consistently demonstrated it to be the case. A Christian must never play the fatalist, even though his academic training or personal inclination might incline him to do so. Neither our tradition nor our Lord gives us that right.

For this reason, I want to suggest three tasks that I consider the foundation and starting points of the intimate community. They do not constitute the totality of such a community, but they are, I think, a place to begin. I will call them a trilogy of concern.

Prayer

However widely you decide to define your enlarged family, commit yourself to pray daily for every member. I realize that, on the surface, this suggestion seems trite and unimaginative. Nevertheless, it is supremely important. I believe, in fact, that it is the single most crucial element in any attempt to bring the expanded family into fruition.

It is important, in the first place, because prayer is effectual. It pleases God to respond to our prayers. This is fortunate, because we who seek to establish the intimate community are waging a war against the powers and principalities of this world. Modern society has aligned its social, political, and economic forces squarely against us. That is the clear implication of the first half of this book. We cannot possibly contest these forces by dint of will power alone. To use a biblical metaphor, we will need to wear the full armor of the Lord. And our chief source of armament is prayer.

My grandmother accomplished a most amazing thing in the modern world. She had four children, all of whom married and had numerous children of their own. Even though her husband had Parkinson's disease for many years (and died when she was only sixty), until she was well into her eighties she invited her children's families over for chicken dinner every Sunday afternoon. Now the amazing thing to me is not only that she had the stamina to perform this task each week, but also that her children, grandchildren, and great-grandchildren delighted in the event. They loved her. They loved each other. They loved to laugh, listen, and debate with one another every Sunday. And they *really* loved her chicken.

I was, of course, one of those grandchildren. Growing up, I assumed everyone regularly enjoyed such family events. Unaware of modernity's impact on grandmas and Sunday afternoons, I thought everyone gobbled up chicken legs and family relationships after church. But now, as I ponder the absolutely peculiar nature of those Sunday afternoons, my mind is drawn irrevocably to another feature of my grandmother's life: prayer. I remember especially those nights when I would stay over at her house. She would tuck me into bed in the front room at around 8:00 or 9:00 and

257

then retire to the back bedroom. Often, an hour or two later, I would be awakened by the anguished voice of my grandmother, pleading to God concerning the lives of each and every member of her family. Friends often told me that our family was lucky— lucky to be together, lucky to enjoy each other's company, lucky to pluck the fruit of such a loving community. In my stupidity, I believed them. But I am convinced that the love in our family was no mystery to God. Nor to my grandmother. Nor can it be to anyone who truly desires the intimate community.

The effect of prayer, however, is not limited to its intended object. Indeed, the most significant consequence of prayer is its effect on the supplicant. God could, after all, respond to the righteous desires of his people regardless of whether or not they were brought before him in prayer. At times, in fact, he does just that. But he commands us to pray, not merely so that he can answer prayer, but so that our relationship with him will mature and our will conform more closely to his. That is, so that we might become more like Christ.

Let me be more concrete. When, in the quiet of the morning, I pray for someone (such as a member of my family), I am engaged in a supremely selfless act. Unlike an offer of time or riches, there is no material reward for intercessory prayer—no word of thanks, no pat on the back, no prestige in the eyes of fellow believers. The prayer for another is a gift of love, without the slightest hint of selfish ambition. It may be the quintessential Christlike act. Little wonder, then, that our love for others deepens as we pray for them, and conversely, we are compelled to pray for those about whom we greatly care. In this equation, too, is the reason we moderns find it so difficult to pray: we are a supremely self-centered people. Who in this narcissistic age is willing spend an hour on his knees, pleading for another, without hope of earthly reward? We are a prayerless generation, not because our schedules are too crowded, but because they have no room for anything as singularly selfless as prayer.

For the expanded family, the chief benefit of intercessory prayer is that it cultivates relationships predicated on love. In the modern era, the expanded family will occur only to the extent that its relationships are based on mutual commitments. Such commitments do not exist because of hopes, dreams, or positive thinking. They exist only as an outgrowth of love. And love is the fruit of prayer.

Communication

If prayer is the foundation of family relationships, communication is its lifeblood. Relationships do not exist in a vacuum. They are dependent on communication for their vitality and depth. One may conceive of one's family in an expanded sense, but if that concept does not result in communication, it is nothing more than a dead concept.

Communication, unfortunately, is a much-abused term in the modern world; it carries with it implications that are neither helpful nor central to our concern. Some readers, for example, will assume something "heavy," or "revealing," or "extraordinary" by the term—as if communication takes place only when secrets are revealed or tears are shed. I, however, assume no such thing. In fact, most communication is mundane and rather matter-of-fact. The modern preoccupation with "spilling one's guts" comes less from the desire to communicate than to "understand" the self. That is why it often takes place in front of strangers (therapists and therapy groups, for example) as well as an anonymous public (movie-goers and readers). Such behavior has little to do with communication.

Others, however, seem to believe that any form of verbal diarrhea constitutes communication. I have been in conversations (so-called) in which individuals carried off perfect imitations of a babbling brook, lacking only its beauty and grace. Such rhetorical displays may, once again, be good for the rhetorician, but they are good for little else. Certainly, they have nothing whatsoever to do with communication.

By communication we simply mean a bilateral exchange of information. It involves passing along and receiving news of people, places, and events. It results in knowledge of another's situation, and another's knowledge of your situation. The substance of this knowledge will range from the lighthearted ("Johnny split his pants in the most embarrassing place!") to the tragic ("Mother—Johnny is gone!"), from the mundane to the morbid. The point of this suggestion is not to define the content of communication, but to make sure it takes place.

Communication is important because it is a precursor to involvement. If I do not understand what is going on in your life, if you do not know what is happening in mine, then we cannot possibly function as a family. Once again, I realize the perfunctory nature of this observation. And yet it must be stated and restated in the modern world. Many of us who like to think of our families in the broadest possible terms fail to communicate anything beyond fundamental rites of passage. But announcements of births, marriages, and wakes do not communication make. Unless we are able to get beyond the "big event" mentality, we will never get into one another's lives.

This failure of communication in the modern world is a curious phenomenon. For we moderns have in our possession unlimited means of communication. Postal services and phone systems—not to mention planes, cars, boats, and trains (although I just did)—

should all serve to make us a more communicative people. We are not communicative, however, primarily because we lack the relationships within which to communicate. The technology that multiplies the possibilities of communication also multiplies the possibilities of relational choice; and, for some reason, we find choices more attractive than communication. As a result, although we have telephone lines in abundance, genuine lines of communication are few and far between.

The intimate community, however, must buck the trend. Indeed, it will survive only if its members engage in frequent communication. The posting of announcements will not do. Neither will the Christmas card, the Easter chocolate, or the birthday wish. Those who hope to function as a family will need to know the warp and woof of one another's lives. That will require frequent contact and interaction. Without it, there will be no involvement. Without it, prayers will have no content, and love will have no meaning. Without it, there will be no intimate community.

Accountability

Finally, there must be the willingness to act on information received. Communication finds its *raison d'etre* in action. Action is its target. Its purpose. Communication, after all, is a means to an end, not an end in itself. To know that your brother is in trouble is of no use if you are unwilling to be of assistance. Communication binds me to my brother only when it is coupled with the will to be my brother's keeper.

I was made painfully aware of the potential hiatus between knowing and doing only yesterday. It was Sunday and, as is our custom, when we arrived at church, I pulled the car up to the front steps to let my family out of the car before attempting to find a parking place. As my son broke for the church door, I noticed that he was carrying his belt in his hands. In a burst of righteous indignation I yelled out, "Your belt won't do you a bit of good if you carry it around all day! Put it on!" Promptly, he complied with my "request."

With a sense of accomplishment, I then proceeded to find a parking place along the side of the road. Unfortunately, I forgot how narrow the road was, and without looking in my rear view mirror, opened my door directly into the path of traffic. One car had to swerve quickly to avoid the opening door, thereby nearly colliding with another car approaching from the opposite direction. Thankfully, an accident was avoided. However, the man who swerved to miss me, promptly stopped his car and gave me the lecture of his life. (It began, interestingly enough, with the words, "Jesus Christ, you'd better get into that church and pray, because you almost killed me!!") In my mind, however, I heard—not the man's lecture—but the imaginary voice of my son saying, "Dad, your brain won't do you a bit of good if you just carry it around with you all day! Use it!"

Since the Fall, I suspect, the gap between knowing and doing has been a perennial human problem. In the modern world, however, it is especially problematic, largely because we moderns are constantly bombarded with knowledge that we cannot immediately use and for which there is often no obvious application. Every evening, as we watch the news, we get hit with a brief slice of life, teeming with action but totally devoid of historical or cultural context. What are we supposed to do with such information? For the first twenty-one years of our lives we sit passively in our chairs, imbibing knowledge, and receiving an education. And what are we supposed to do with this knowledge? The scientist who wants to earn the plaudits of his peer, is required to do his research in a dispassionate, value-free manner. But what is he supposed to *do* with his findings?

There are, of course, modern answers to these questions. Ahistorical bits of news are supposed to produce a better-informed citizenry. Twenty-one years of "information gathering" is supposed to land us a better job. And the passionless scientist is supposed to be a better scientist. Whatever truth there may be in these assertions (and I have significant questions about them all), of one thing I am certain: We have become accustomed to receiving information without the slightest expectation that we will immediately put it to use. Hence, we have learned to divorce knowledge from its personal implications.

Those who desire the intimate community, however, must learn a different truth—that knowing without doing is a very dangerous thing. Nothing will fracture the family more than knowledge without accountability. When we see our brother stumble, we must help him to stand. When we hear that our brother is lost, we must seek him out and set him on the right path. When we learn that our brother has triumphed, we must rejoice with him in his accomplishment. When our brother is in pain, we must share his tears. In his joy we must rejoice; in his laughter we must laugh. For that which we know of our brother, we must hold ourselves accountable.

What we must not do is gossip. Gossip, of course, is nothing more than knowledge for which we assume no accountability. It is information about someone—information that passes from speaker to hearer without a hint of application or use. Gossip enables us to delight in the hearing without feeling any obligation to respond. That is why gossip is often full of errors: it forever escapes the test of reality. That is why gossip is evil: its orbit is always outside the realm of truth. When brother gossips against brother, he claims the right to distance himself, not only from truth, but also from his brother. With every irresponsible word, accountability fades and the distance between brothers grows. Gossip gives way to slander, which in turn breeds suspicion, anger, and hatred. When accountability dies, the death of the intimate community is sure.

Am I my brother's keeper? The world in which we exist sometimes says yes, but always lives the no. Cain also assumed that the answer was no—at least his actions assumed it. What do we assume? When the Lord of creation asks us, "Where is Abel, your brother?" how do we respond? Do we know? Do we care? On our answer, I am convinced, hangs the fate of the modern family.

CONCLUSION: MINOR THOUGHTS AND SUGGESTIONS

Mutual commitments; hard questions for modernity; an expanded-family concept injected with prayer, communication, and accountability—these, I believe, are the rudiments of the intimate community. In them there is nothing easy. But for that I do not apologize. In the environment of modernity, simple formulas or pat techniques may flourish for a season, but they are destined to wither and decay. It is only through the persistence of God's people—and his grace—that the intimate community may one day bear fruit.

Before concluding, however, I would like to offer a few minor thoughts and suggestions. They are minor because they are relatively unimportant. They will neither ensure success nor carry one through the conflagrations of modernity. If one is determined to walk in the right direction, however, they just might boost one over a hurdle or two—and possibly even help avoid a wrong turn along the way.

1. Develop and keep family traditions

Repeatedly, I have stressed that traditions are the keepers of the past, for good or ill. Assuming that family relationships are one of the "goods," it would behoove us to develop and sustain family traditions.

How this is done, of course, depends on circumstances, but I suggest that daily, weekly, monthly, and yearly traditions be established. In our family, for example, we have turned the evening meal into a daily tradition that includes togetherness during food preparation, a prayer of thanks, eating the food and discussing the day's events, and finally a time of reading. "Reading time" takes thirty minutes to an hour and enables us, as a family, to digest, not only our food but also the best literature the English language has to offer. Keeping this tradition is not always easy, but it is rewarding. It is a tradition of togetherness.

Sundays, birthdays, holy days, seasons, and festivals can all be turned into meaningful traditions. But holidays do not make a tradition. Turning Christmas into a tradition that is both Christian and togetherness- oriented, for example, takes planning and persistence. If the expanded family is to become a reality, moreover, some of these traditions ought to include more than just the nuclear family.

2. Select family roles and carry them out

I am of the opinion that, in the modern world, role confusion is a far more significant matter than role playing. Whether parents decide to establish a democratic, a patriarchal, or a matriarchal family is not especially interesting to me. As long as such patterns operate within the context of Christian norms, most are quite workable. In saying this, I risk incurring the wrath of both the right and left. So be it. Those who think that any particular authority pattern by itself will solve relational problems within the family are buying into a modern myth. They are greatly deceived.

What does concern me, however, is the proliferation of families without well-defined role relationships. The family cannot be a source of security and solidarity if its members are constantly vying for position. Such competition merely brings the modern fascination with "choice" into the midst of family relationships. Choices must be made, to be sure, but they should be made before, not after, the family has been established. I would suggest, therefore, that brides and grooms discuss this matter before their wedding date, develop a "role model" to follow, and then work out the kinks in that model during the first few years of marriage (in fear and trembling, I might add). After that, get on with *being* a family. Given the modern preoccupation with alternatives, this will not be easy. But it will be rewarding.

3. Denuke the modern family

Many who read these pages are presently part of a nuclear family, with little hope of expanding the perimeters of that family. Even if they apply our rule of thumb, they will not have a nonnuclear family for ten to twenty years. Is there nothing they can do in the meantime to broaden their family's horizons?

A good way to denuke the modern family is through adoption—not in the formal sense, maybe, but by common agreement. This can take many forms. Two or three nuclear families might want to adopt one another and form an expanded family. Less radical would be to adopt one or two people in your church or community, preferably those who are different from you and in need of family relationships. Widows or widowers, an older couple without children nearby, singles of any age, someone of a different economic or racial background, a prisoner in a nearby penal institution—the possibilities are endless. Whatever the choice, and whatever the details of such an arrangement, commit yourself to the trilogy of concern: pray for one another, communicate regularly, and be accountable for one another.

Because the adopted family exists by virtue of choice rather than birth, it will not duplicate the intimate community. But it can be a very special community—one that will stretch the hearts and minds of its members, and provide a social bond where none existed before. And that is no mean accomplishment in the modern world.

4. Make modernity a matter of discussion

A point I have repeatedly made throughout this book is that if modernity offers a significant challenge to community, then those who desire the intimate community must constantly question the values of our age. But the question is, How? While there can be no easy answer to this question, let me offer a suggestion.

Within the family, make modern values and assumptions a matter of discussion and debate. Television, newspapers, movies, and sometimes sermons and lectures are teeming with modern assumptions. Challenge them—out loud and with other family members. When you are watching an advertisement on TV and a voice proclaims that some product will make you wonderful or wise, extend your tongue and give it the raspberries. When a preacher suggests that he has some clever technique to make the church grow or make you happy, don't give him the raspberries, give him the Word and make his assumption a matter of discussion at dinner. When listening to a song with lyrics that declare, "It can't be wrong, if it feels so right," shake your head in amazement and tell your world, "You lose, Debbie. It's wrong if it's wrong—period."

Whatever you do and however you decide to approach the problem, do not let modern assertions go unchallenged. Otherwise, the distinction between knowing and doing is encouraged, and the delusions of modernity become your own. We cannot (and should not) cut ourselves off from modernity; it is our world and to it we have a responsibility. But neither can we let its values become our standards nor allow its assumptions to parade as truth. Rather, together we must challenge modernity, in word as well as deed.

5. *Live the message spoken*

In the final analysis, however, words alone will not bring about the intimate community. It will take deeds—many of them—in concert with a multitude of deeds from other like-minded individuals. If all we do is verbally challenge modernity, we may become good critics, but we will not change our world.

For that, we must emulate the way of our Lord. He was a Teacher, yes, and his Word still reverberates in the hearts and minds of his people. But his teaching was always informed by action. And so, for his ministry, he selected twelve rather unimpressive chaps to walk with him and learn his ways. It was a small community—but it changed human history. As the disciples daily listened to the teachings of Jesus, they were routinely amazed as well as confused. But they learned from his life—his healing, rebuking, forgiving, and loving—that his Word was worth remembering, even when they failed to understand it. And when did they finally understand the meaning of Christ's message? When he gave up his life for them—and us— and then overcame death itself. In that event, in the actions of their Savior, they suddenly understood the radical implications of his Word.

The modern world will not comprehend our words either. The words of those who value relationships

with God and other human beings will not be understood by those who live for self. Our words will appear bizarre and out of place, strange utterances in a
world of strangers. The actions of those who value
community will also appear odd, of course. But they
will be different from words because their peculiarity
cannot be ignored. In a world of empty rhetoric,
words can be easily dismissed. But actions cannot. Actions grate, unnerve, and challenge the status quo. We
can talk about community until the cows come home,
and little will come of it. Or, we can act on the assumption that people are more important than
self-gratification, and change our world.

PART VII / Modernity at Bay: Community Expressed

seventeen / The Practice of Community

I have an acquaintance who makes his living traveling around the country, speaking to audiences interested in his message. The exact nature of his profession, along with the content of his speeches, is irrelevant. The important thing is that he goes from town to town, making predictable speeches and eliciting predictable responses. It is an experience, he confesses, that is not altogether fulfilling. The problem, he says, is that he finds it difficult to think of his audience as ordinary people. Rather, they are like instruments that must be properly tuned, stroked, and plucked. If he performs his task well, they respond with beautiful music (and not a small amount of cash). If he should conduct himself poorly, however, he knows a new musician will be found.

It seems to me that nothing captures the essence of modernity like the professional traveler. Whether it's the artist who conducts a series of one-night stands or the politician who repeats the same speech to hundreds of faceless crowds or the salesman who throws the same pitch to an infinite number of nameless faces, the result is identical. The performer and the audience make an exchange of valuables, each hoping to profit from the experience, but neither expecting to form anything like a durable relationship.

For most of us in the modern world, the great preponderance of our relationships are like those of the professional traveler. As we move from place to place, we do not expect to build permanent relationships. Rather, we hope to form alliances and short-term contracts from which we will personally profit. We look at others, not as God's image bearers, but as means to personal gratification. Because this is standard fare in the modern world, we see nothing wrong with such associations. We trust that these alliances will be mutually beneficial and hope that everyone will receive their fair share of gratifying relationships.

But as we have seen, such alliances are not mutually beneficial, and communities based on them are anything but fair. Some among us are better salesmen than others, having more of what is deemed valuable by the modern world (beauty, self-confidence, intelligence, etc.) and therefore find others eager to enter into relationships with them. Others, however, are not good at relational barter. They either lack the resources or social skills to play the modern game of alliance formation. For them, the modern world is not only less than just, it is lonely beyond imagination.

A ROAD LESS TRAVELED

Jesus presented us with a picture of another kind of traveler:

> A man was going down from Jerusalem to Jericho, when he fell into the hands of robbers. They stripped him of his clothes, beat him and went away, leaving him half dead. A priest happened to be going down the same road, and when he saw the man, he passed by on the other side. So too, a Levite, when he came to the place and saw him, passed by on the other side. But a Samaritan, as he traveled, came where the man was; and when he saw him, he took pity on him. He went to him and bandaged his wounds, pouring on oil and wine. Then he put the man on his own donkey, took him to an inn and took care of him. The next day he took out two silver coins and gave them to the innkeeper. "Look after him," he said, "and when I return, I will reimburse you for any extra expense you may have." (Luke 10:30-35).

I noted, early in our journey, that the modern world is annoyed by the Good Samaritan, not by the priest or the Levite. We are irked by the Good Samaritan, not because we fail to appreciate his altruistic act, but because his world is so alien from our own that his actions hardly make sense. From the perspective of modernity, the Samaritan simply did everything wrong.

For one thing, he chose to base his actions on another's need rather than on personal profit. It is easy to identify with the priest and the Levite because they took the path of least personal cost; ignoring the beaten man cost them nothing in prestige (who would know?) or money. Indeed, by ignoring the problem they no doubt maintained their schedule, pleasing those with whom they worked. The Samaritan, on the other hand, delayed his trip and spent a tidy sum, all without a hint of personal profit or gain. From the

perspective of the modern values of efficiency, survival, and self-gratification, the Samaritan was an abysmal
failure.

But he was worse than a failure because he did a
most dangerous thing. He got involved. He shunned
the traveler's cloak of anonymity in order to embrace
the one who was needy. He refused to use mobility
as an excuse for irresponsibility and chose instead to
include the needy in his world. Such an act is dangerous. The man who had been beaten and robbed might
himself have been a robber; he might have repaid the
Good Samaritan with treachery. Those who practice
inclusivity are extremely vulnerable. Their kindness
and generosity is easily exploited. Reason is not on
the side of the Good Samaritan; the reasonable thing
is to avoid risk and all those things that come between us and our objectives. But for the sake of a
greater good, the Samaritan was willing to set aside
the logic of self-preservation.

Despite its danger, despite its cost, despite our inability to fully comprehend it—the Samaritan's act is
radical and world-shaking in its implications. Indeed,
it is precisely because it is dangerous, costly, and incomprehensible that the Samaritan's behavior is revolutionary. It challenges modern sensibilities. It throws
into question the values of self-fulfillment and personal gratification. It heralds the news that there is something more important than profit or efficiency, more
significant than our dreams of other possibilities, more
glorious than any of the choices that modernity
spreads before us.

MODERNITY AT BAY

How can we have community in this age? Like the
Good Samaritan, we must choose it. We must take the
weapon of modernity and use it against itself. Modernity must be hoisted by its own petard.

In some cases, that means choosing not to do what modernity expects or recommends. Choosing not to pass by the one who is in need. Choosing not to give up on relationships because they are embarrassing, or hard, or less than what we dreamed. Choosing not to walk out on churches because they fail to inspire us every Sunday morning. Choosing not to walk out on spouses because they fail to arouse us every night. Choosing not to ignore the weak, the old, and the homeless because they are not a part of the modern definition of the family. Choosing not to dump traditions because they are time consuming or inefficient. Choosing to give up the right of choice.

It will mean, as well, choosing to make the right choice. More than anything else, community in the modern world depends on our willingness to emulate the Samaritan's choice—on our willingness to choose to include, to embrace. To include the lovely as well as the loveless. To embrace those who are blessed with modernity's values as well as those perceived to be valueless. In short, to accept those whom God has placed along our way—not as hindrances to be avoided or helps to be exploited—but as responsibilities to be assumed and as opportunities for community.

It is a difficult choice, to be sure. It was hard enough for Adam and Eve to resist the lure of "other possibilities," even in the best of circumstances. In the wake of their failure and in the context of modernity, the choice may seem impossible. And yet, God is in the business of reconciliation. It was to this end that he sent his Son into the world and it is for this purpose that his Spirit moves among us even now. Trusting in his Son and believing in the power of his Spirit, let us be about our Father's business, knowing that whenever people reach out to others, building bridges over modern chasms, not only do they put modernity at bay, but they split the darkness with the Light of the World.